Praise for *What Does That Mean?*

*"Eldon's provocative voice of wisdom and compassion places his readers right on the dot about the meaning of their individual existence. **What Does That Mean?** reveals how the paradoxes we face in everyday life form the rich material that invites us to confidently enter the mystery and relish it. Read, practice, and celebrate!"*

— **Michael Bernard Beckwith,** author of
Spiritual Liberation—Fulfilling Your Soul's Potential

*"**What Does That Mean?** guides you to ask deeply probing questions that often go ignored but must be examined if you are ever to live your best life possible. Highly recommended."*

— **Marci Shimoff**, #1 *New York Times* best-selling author of *Happy for No Reason* and *Chicken Soup for the Woman's Soul*

"I love this book! There is something about the energetics of Eldon's languaging that breaks open my heart. It's very vulnerable, but if one possesses the courage to fully let it in and respond to it, there is great power involved."

— **Anita Rehker**

*"**What Does That Mean?** goes far beyond 'exploring mind, meaning, and mysteries'! It's a deeply satisfying and divinely inspired book that will not only explain so many uncertainties; it will also heal many a tattered soul. Both scientific and spiritual, strong and soft, spellbinding and soothing . . . this is a must-read!"*

— **Crystal Andrus,** author of *Simply . . . Woman!* and *Transcendent Beauty*

*"I've found all of Eldon Taylor's books fascinating, but **What Does That Mean?** is his magnum opus, offering a rare look at how inner guidance plays out in real life."*

— **Caroline Sutherland,** author of *The Body Knows . . . How to Stay Young*

*"**What Does That Mean?** is engaging, thought provoking, and quite simply a great read!"*

— **Christiane Northrup, M.D.,** author of *The Secret Pleasures of Menopause* and *Women's Bodies, Women's Wisdom*

"Eldon Taylor weaves together spiritual inquiry, self-disclosure, and masterful storytelling to make this insightful book an easy read that's accessible for everyone. Highly recommended."

— **Chuck Hillig,** author of *Enlightenment for Beginners* and *Looking for God*

*"Eldon Taylor is one of the world's most brilliant modern-day philosophers. **What Does That Mean?** is a thought-provoking, engaging read that will capture your attention and have you contemplating every aspect of life itself."*

— **Peggy McColl,** the *New York Times* best-selling author of *Your Destiny Switch*

*"Dream, ponder, think, and most of all revel in the delightful mind treat offered by Eldon Taylor. Sparkling with great stories and great insight, **What Does That Mean?** helps you discover the immense and inherent power in your fascinating mind. Read it and think—truly think—for yourself."*

— **Terri Marie,** CEO, White Wing Entertainment LLC

*". . . In this new work of art by Eldon Taylor, we are blessed to finally have an insight into why we function the way we do and what it means to us. Changing from survival-based creatures to ecstatic beings walking a path of bliss and beauty requires hard work for most of us because we are conditioned differently. Figuring out our reason for being, and indeed the reason for everything, is Eldon's primary focus in this revealing book. "**What Does That Mean?** . . . will gently invite [readers] to deeply question their motives for behaving as they do. Citing situations, studies, personal experiences, and observations over his decades as a pioneering researcher, Eldon lets us know in clear terms what Bjork has been telling us for years: There's definitely no logic to human behavior."*

— **Shazzie,** author of *Detox Your World* and *Ecstatic Being*

*"**What Does That Mean?** makes the profound case that through the intelligent examination of our assumptions and beliefs, we can find the answers to the quintessential questions of our time: 'What is the meaning of life?' 'What is my role?' and 'What the heck do I need to do to make a difference now?' This book inspires readers to question everything they hold to be 'true,' examine where we, as a society, have allowed our moral compass to be derailed, and what we need to do to course-correct immediately. Through the inquisition of his soul's pondering, Eldon shares his journey of fulfillment and purpose in a way that is accessible, authentic, and practical enough for readers to follow suit. This is a refreshingly inspiring and motivating book!"*

— **Anisa Aven,** author, conscious entrepreneur, and spiritual activist

*"Thoughtful, provocative, insightful, and fascinating, Dr. Eldon Taylor's **What Does That Mean?** explores the meaning of life and enlightenment from many perspectives and disciplines. Great insights await those willing to ponder the many questions he offers, all filled with wisdom. I highly recommend this intelligent and mind-expanding book."*

— **Dr. Joe Rubino,** CEO, **CenterForPersonalReinvention.com** and creator, **SelfEsteemSystem.com**

"Taking examples from his life and the lives of others, Dr. Eldon Taylor reminds us that we experience life in 'shades of gray,' something that gives us due cause to stop and ponder the meaning of these experiences. Eldon asserts that life is about questions, and he ends most chapters with the query 'What does that mean?'—the title of the book. As one reads this excellent work, it becomes clear that the answer is actually hidden in the question! In this book, we're reminded that in our quest for enlightenment, we must look within and we must incorporate mind, body . . . and spirit. I recommend this book for the seeker, a person who questions life and the nature of reality."

— **John L. Turner, M.D.,** author of *Medicine, Miracles, & Manifestations*

"As Eldon Taylor exposes emotional events in his life, he invites readers to examine their own stories for underlying meanings that left lasting impressions. These personal-growth benchmarks are embedded in the memories of encounters with strangers, family members, and friends, sometimes surprisingly. A thought-provoking, insightful book that demands our personal involvement in understanding why we think what we think and what it all means. Bravo!"

— **Elaine Smitha,** author of *If You Make The Rules,*
How Come You're Not Boss?

"I found Eldon Taylor's most thought-provoking book to date, **What Does That Mean?**, to be an empirical and personally resonant ride through the maze of human experience and soul evolution. It takes a lot of courage to fillet yourself and truly examine both your spirit and your humanness; and at the end of your inspection, discover that your life of questing and experience still leaves you with even more unanswered questions. But it's the very exploration and search for meaning that compels us to push our boundaries into new self-discovery. The truth is that it's a magnificent ride that never ends!"

— **Angelina Heart,** author of *The Teaching of Little Crow*
and the audio-educational series *Twin Flames*

"The quality of your life may well be a function of the questions you ask yourself. Enlightenment, like happiness, is found within. If you lost your memory, would you still be you? Not who you think you are, but the essential you? Would you be the real you without having those memories? You may ask: What does that mean? It means you should read Eldon Taylor's book by that title and start to ask yourself the right questions. As Socrates said: 'The unexamined life is not worth living.' Life gives you lessons. Asking the right questions can lead you to the head of the class."

— **Lionel Ketchian,** founder of **HappinessClub.com**

"I am grateful for Eldon's willingness to share his journey into meaning. I am convinced **What Does That Mean?** will deepen every reader's own journey into their understanding of meaning in their lives."

— **Doreen Banaszak,** author of *Excuse Me, Your Life Is Now*

What Does That Mean?

Also by Eldon Taylor

*Choices and Illusions: How Did I Get Where I Am,
and How Do I Get Where I Want to Be?**

Exclusively Fabricated Illusions

Just Be: A Little Cowboy Philosophy

Little Black Book

*Mind Programming: From Persuasion and Brainwashing to
Self-Help and Practical Metaphysics**

Simple Things and Simple Thoughts

Subliminal Communication: Emperor's Clothes or Panacea?

Subliminal Learning: An Eclectic Approach

Subliminal Technology: Unlocking the Power of Your Own Mind

Thinking Without Thinking: Who's in Control of Your Mind?

Wellness: Just a State of Mind?

Plus hundreds of audio and video programs in multiple languages

*Available from Hay House

Please visit Hay House USA: **www.hayhouse.com**®
Hay House Australia: **www.hayhouse.com.au**
Hay House UK: **www.hayhouse.co.uk**
Hay House South Africa: **www.hayhouse.co.za**
Hay House India: **www.hayhouse.co.in**

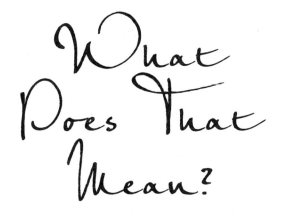

What Does That Mean?

Exploring
Mind, Meaning,
and Mysteries

ELDON TAYLOR

HAY HOUSE, INC.
Carlsbad, California • New York City
London • Sydney • Johannesburg
Vancouver • Hong Kong • New Delhi

Published and distributed in the United States by: Hay House, Inc.: www.hayhouse
.com • *Published and distributed in Australia by:* Hay House Australia Pty. Ltd.: www
.hayhouse.com.au • *Published and distributed in the United Kingdom by:* Hay House
UK, Ltd.: www.hayhouse.co.uk • *Published and distributed in the Republic of South
Africa by:* Hay House SA (Pty), Ltd.: www.hayhouse.co.za • *Distributed in Canada by:*
Raincoast: www.raincoast.com • *Published in India by:* Hay House Publishers India:
www.hayhouse.co.in

Editorial supervision: Jill Kramer • *Project Editor:* Jessica Kelley • *Design:* Jami Goddess
Eldon Taylor's editor: Suzanne Brady

Library of Congress Cataloging-in-Publication Data

Taylor, Eldon.
  What does that mean? : exploring mind, meaning, and mysteries / Eldon Taylor. --
1st ed.
     p. cm.
  ISBN 978-1-4019-2333-4 (hardcover : alk. paper) 1. Life--Miscellanea. I. Title.
BF1999.T315 2010
128--dc22

                              2009023681

ISBN: 978-1-4019-2333-4

13 12 11 10   4 3 2 1
1st edition, January 2010

Printed in the United States of America

For the past 20 years, I've enjoyed daily conversations that have clarified and improved my thinking. Usually over the dining room table and a cup of coffee, and sometimes for hours, these talks have deeply enriched my life. They usually start with a simple question—at least it seems simple in the beginning.

To Ravinder, my conversational friend, wife, and partner, who without fail or fault has stood beside me through all sorts of personal and professional—shall we say, opportunities— and to whom I am forever grateful, this book is for you.

Contents

A New Day

This is the beginning of a new day.
I have been given this day to use as I will.
I can waste it or use it for good.
<u>What I do today is important because</u>
<u>I'm exchanging a day of my life for it.</u>
When tomorrow comes, this day will be gone forever,
leaving in its place whatever I have traded it for.
I pledge to myself that it shall be . . .
Gain, not loss
Good, not evil
Success, not failure
In order that I shall not regret the price I paid for this day.

— Anonymous

Foreword

It was 11 o'clock in the evening, but I couldn't put down this book until I'd finished the last page. Then I stood up and slid open the door to my backyard. As I inhaled the fresh evening air, the energy of the book flowed through me. It reveals author Eldon Taylor at his best. After elegantly and eloquently leading readers into understanding the mysteries of the conscious and subconscious mind in his previous two books, *Choices and Illusions* and *Mind Programming,* Eldon again proves his mastery of the mind in this latest volume, *What Does That Mean?*

This book is definitely the crown jewel of his trilogy. Provoking an inner dialogue regarding the true meaning of life, the author invites you to ask questions, to become more curious, to notice coincidences in your daily life, and then gradually to undertake a profound analysis of ways to know your own inner self.

Eldon keeps your attention focused by slowly increasing both the complexity of the topics he discusses and the depth of his analysis as he speaks to novices and laypeople alike. I imagine you'll feel as I do— that Eldon shows the eternal human facing the mystery of existence, humbled by the beauty and the complexity of one's own life journey. He understands that it's much easier to advance spiritually once you've been awakened. Proving himself profoundly knowledgeable about human nature, he gives you practical tools you'll need in your own quest for answers. That is perhaps the most powerful gift of all his books. He'll impress you with the consistency of his discourse and his profound love for the human race.

Eldon is widely known as a leader of thought, a leader in character formation, a visionary. His books and his extremely efficient subliminal InnerTalk programs continue to contribute significantly to the development and advancement of the human race.

— **Cristian Enescu, M.D.**

Introduction

"*The outward work will never be puny if the inward work is great.*"
— **Meister Eckhart**

The primary person I'm thinking about while writing and sharing this work with you—is *you*. My life has unfolded in surprising yet common ways, and often I've simply overlooked the obvious. My experience suggests that I'm not alone, for most of us dismiss the conspicuous and sometimes even the most important thing—the very meaning of life.

It seems trite to suggest that an inquiry into the meaning of life is justified. After all, that's the subject of religions, spiritual gurus, and even life coaches and psychologists; it's everywhere. That's true, but unlike most volumes that are on the shelves of your local bookstore, I don't claim to tell you any great secret. No, indeed. Rather, I'll ask you to think about what you believe, to examine the common things in everyday life and ask: What does that mean?

Most individuals reach a point in their lives when they look back at their experiences and wonder, *What's it all about?* This question underlies the values of all humankind.

Events, and even more lessons and thoughts, have led me to ask this very thing many times. For example, I once had a dream that warned me of something. Indeed, it awakened me, and I discovered that the fire I'd dreamed about was just starting in my kitchen. I put out the flames and then sat down and reflected on the entire experience. My left-brain analysis suggested that I'd remembered, at some level of my being, leaving the burner on and a kitchen towel near it. My right-brain evaluation was entirely different. A power had awakened me, perhaps a spiritual guide or something similar, but whatever the source, it wasn't just my mind doing the job. I asked myself, *What does that mean?*

Many of us ask this question, especially when we're reflecting on matters that challenge typical explanations. We experience this sort of thing more often than we might think. We're a conscious, thinking species that takes great pride in our large brains and how we use them. The brain sets us apart from the other life-forms that inhabit our planet—or so we think. If that's the case, and we fail to use our brains, then our perception of the world is little different from that of a lower animal, such as a monkey. Then again, it has been said, "God plagued man with the ability to think." So which way is it? Is it fair to ask, *What does that mean?*

So many people today have lost the ability to think and have unknowingly given over their minds to the media, to their peers, and to society. The result is that they're the product of the collective mind programming that dictates the clothes they wear, the way they stand, the places where they shop, their dreams of success, the goals they pursue, and more. A special form of brainwashing has taken place.

In many cases, bumper-sticker mottoes have become our beliefs, and we behave accordingly. "It's okay to get even" and "Go ahead and make my day" become principles we adopt, expectations we plan for, latent hostility we cling to, and so forth. We're brainwashed by opinions—everyone's opinions—but how about yours? Who are *you*, after all?

I've asked this question often and continue to do so. Some insights have come from life itself. The adventures I've lived and that I share with you in this book are all true. They may challenge your beliefs, as they did mine. I hope you'll relate to some of them at least, and reading my accounts may refresh your memory about things that happened to you. I believe that everyone's life tells a unique story. Your purpose is in that story and your adventures, just as it's in your passions and fears.

In my previous two books, *Choices and Illusions* and *Mind Programming,* I hope I showed just how much of our thinking has been foisted upon us, and how little original thinking each of us truly experiences. So many of the ideas we believe to be our own really don't stand up to even superficial examination.

It's my intent in this book to share anecdotes, stories, and insights that invariably lead to questions that aren't easily answered. Each chapter presents thought-provoking and sometimes controversial topics that are often ignored. It's my wish that you pause at the conclusion of each chapter to reflect upon its content and implied possibilities. Ideally, you'll write your own notes, recording what arises as a result of your feelings and thoughts regarding each chapter.

You should know that although I'll repeatedly be asking the question: *What does that mean?* I won't be providing answers. It's imperative, in my opinion, that you come to your own thoughtful conclusions; for the purpose of this work is, after all, to provoke the endeavor known as "thoughtful inquiry."

I hope to provoke your mental processes with this book, and I truly would like your thoughts in return. I hope you'll go to my Website: **www.eldontaylor.com** and participate in my *What Does That Mean?* blog. Together we can better understand each other and the world we share. In the process, I hope you'll gain some inkling as to what your own life is truly about and thereby begin the process of finding yourself.

chapter 1

WHAT DOES THAT MEAN?

*"The miracle is not to fly in the air, or to walk
on the water, but to walk on the earth."*
— **Chinese proverb**

One night as I drifted off to sleep, I reflected on unexplained events in my life and wondered, *What does that mean?* The next morning as I dressed, I heard someone on the television in the next room saying, "It's amazing. The window washer fell 500 feet, and he lived. That story and more, next." I asked myself, *What does that mean? What does it mean to the window washer?*

That day as I drove home from the grocery store, I noticed a young man and his child. The weather was finally springlike, and this fellow was working in a tiny garden. He appeared to be breaking up some small clods by repeated blows with a hoe. I thought back to my first home and garden. Such pride, such ambition—and such is the great American dream. In the United States, most of us plan on owning our own little piece of heaven; after all, a man's home is his castle. As young people, we plan to buy our first vehicle, and the consumption cycle begins. (Oh, we're consuming prior to that, but for most of us it's limited to what the family provides, and because my point has

1

nothing to do with when or how the consumption habit begins, I'll just leave it at that.)

So we make our plans, our dreams, and begin to live them out to the best of our ability. Our clothes, automobiles, homes, furniture, group memberships, and so on are all a part of our dreams. The food we eat, the stops at Starbucks for a fancy latte, the cell phones we carry, and on and on are also part of our dreams. I could go on, but let's consider another way to look at this dream. Are we consuming, or are we being consumed?

Is there a *"now"* moment where the heart is not just beating, as Henry Wadsworth Longfellow says:

> *And our hearts, though stout and brave,*
> *Still, like muffled drums, are beating*
> *Funeral marches to the grave.*

Life has many twists and turns, and seldom do we find the road to be straight and narrow. The same can be said for the choices we have to make as well. We are sometimes tossed about like leaves in a windstorm, bouncing from one event to the next, and—despite our efforts to take control—unable to shut down the prevailing winds. In the midst of all of this, we can find ourselves experiencing the seemingly impossible. Why? How does that happen? And what does it mean?

The Train Accident

When I was just 17 years old, I was driving a car that stalled on a set of railroad tracks. My side of the vehicle was facing an oncoming train traveling approximately 100 miles per hour and pulling more than 100 cars. The young lady who was with me, her hand on my leg, watched while I tried to start the car so that I could drive it off the tracks. But in what seemed no time at all, the train struck the car. The driver's side was crushed under the cowcatcher (the slanted piece on the lower front of the engine) as the train dragged the car down the tracks and finally threw the wreckage into a weedy field next to the tracks.

My friend Connie was cut from the car with a welder's torch. She asked about me while they worked to get her free, but they told her nothing. Bless her heart, she also worried that her new nylon stockings might have been damaged. Shock often has a disorienting effect such as that.

As for me, I found myself standing a few hundred feet away in the field. Suddenly, as if dropped there and awakened, I looked around to see all kinds of emergency vehicles, other automobiles, and a crowd of onlookers. I hurried toward the ambulance but was stopped by emergency crew members. They wanted to know who I was, since from my location and appearance, I clearly couldn't have been involved in the accident.

This experience affected my life in many ways. One of those, and perhaps the most meaningful, is the spiritual element. Either a miracle had occurred or I was dead. Connie knew I was in the car when it was struck. How did I live?

I told this story in my earlier book *Choices and Illusions*. Readers have written to tell me of similar events in their lives. Here is one of them (used by permission):

> Last night I read in your book the story about the train wreck and how you found yourself feet away from the accident site. I had a similar experience in Southern California. I was on the on-ramp to the freeway. At this particular entrance, cars also came off the freeway, and I had to look to my right to ensure I had room and that a vehicle wasn't coming at me. In front of me was a big truck, and I was driving a small, subcompact car. In an instant, the truck in front of me hit his brakes. I had nowhere to go and should have ended up under the truck. Yet through some strange turn of events, I found myself in a lane on the freeway, driving 60 miles an hour. There was no way I could have done that!

I was totally shaken over the episode and thankful that I'd received the help of whatever or whoever put me in a safe place. It almost felt as if time and space were shifted to have me where I needed to be, out of harm's way. In that moment, I knew there are laws and explanations we don't seem to have if we only see ourselves as one-dimensional limited beings.

Thank you for letting me share this story. I'd never heard of someone having a similar experience until I read your book Choices and Illusions.

So what does all this mean? What does it signify when life hands us the unexplained? What about when the wisdom of our culture crashes down on broken promises and failed dreams? What does it mean when our spiritual or scientific models collapse under the weight of real-life observation and experience? Is any of this really possible, or is it just a point of view, a place of perspective, an expectation self-fulfilled?

Approaching the Many-Worlds Argument

I have a very bright son—more than one, actually—but the one I'm referring to has changed his colors many times as he has grown into his teenage years. He is named after my dear friend Roy Bey, whom I shall tell you more about during the course of this book, but who has passed on. My son Roy adopted Catholicism last year and he pushed us to attend the Catholic church. This year, however, he's agnostic to atheist. He likes to think of himself as a six on the scale of the renowned atheist Richard Dawkins, and that means he is agnostic, for he doesn't believe there is a God, and he lives his life according to that belief. He also thinks it isn't possible to be sure about the divine either way, so he can't say with absolute certainty that there is no God, and as such he can't claim to be atheist!

Our recent conversations have often been focused on Freud, particularly his psychosexual development theories, and Dawkins, the author of *The God Delusion*. When Roy gets an idea in his head, it's

4

imperative that he both share it and convince others of its worthiness. So if you're not inclined toward his kind of agnosticism, then it's his challenge to convince you of your error.

There have been many of what I'd call "miracles" in my life, and my agnostic son, Roy, knows of most of them. I brought up this topic, saying: "If there are no miracles in the world, then perhaps there's no evidence that can't be explained away by science. If there *are* miracles in the world, however, then perhaps you should rethink your position. For example, how would you explain the train wreck when I was a teenager?"

His answer, in brief, was: "Simple, Dad. It was a quantum jump."

We know about electron jumps—like them, my train-wreck experience was just a function of natural law that we have yet to understand. It all has to do with the many-worlds argument and dimensions.

The Garden in the Jungle

The many-worlds argument, quantum jumps, yet-to-be-discovered natural laws—all are reminiscent to me of an old Antony Flew analogy. Flew, a philosopher intellectual, suggested what's generally referred to as "the gardener story," or "the falsification debate." Loosely and admittedly with some exaggeration, the story goes like this: Imagine that two fellows happen upon a garden in the middle of a jungle. The plot appears to be very well kept: Corn, squash, carrots, peas, and so forth grow in straight rows. There are no weeds. The compost windrows are not only straight, but appear to be groomed.

Now, our two gentlemen have different views about this garden. The first man (I'll call him Believer, or "B" for short) says, "What a nice garden. I wonder where the gardener is."

The second (I'll call him Doubter, or just "D") says, "There is no gardener. This is a natural part of the world. Like so many other perfect relationships in nature, this is a wonder, but it's totally natural."

Here are two opposing views of the same thing. B replies, "You have to be kidding. Look at the crops in the garden: they all grow in straight rows. Look at the weeds: there simply are none. Look at the compost windrows: you can see where they've recently been groomed with a rake."

D answers, "It's just like you to anthropomorphize everything. I suppose someone placed the stars in the sky in exactly the right way to create the Big and the Little Dippers. Look—everything in this natural area you call a garden is no more than a special type of oasis in the midst of a jungle. You wouldn't peer over a giant sand dune in the desert and argue that the oasis below was created by an oasis builder—or would you?"

B, speaking in a rather annoyed tone, says, "All right. Let's wait and see. I'll show you that there's a gardener. We'll hide; and when the gardener comes back, you'll have your proof. How's that?"

D, just as annoyed, replies, "Fine. That's just fine, but what if he doesn't ever appear? Then will you admit there's no gardener?"

No gardener ever comes. B argues that perhaps the person is invisible, so D installs an electric fence and takes guard dogs to the premises, but no one shows up. The crops still grow in straight lines, no weeds sprout, and the windrows continue to appear to be tended. All this, yet still no gardener.

B continues to believe, and finally D asks the big (and baited) question: "What would it take to convince you that there's no gardener?"

B answers, "There must be one. Just because we haven't seen or touched him, the dogs haven't smelled him, and so forth, doesn't mean he doesn't exist!"

D presents the argument of the empiricist, and the belief of B is ridiculed in light of the lack of observable evidence. However, the argument works the other way as well. Take my son Roy, whom I asked: "Are there miracles in the world?" If everything is only a matter of an as-yet-undiscovered natural law, then there are no miracles, and nothing can prove otherwise. The definition contains the subject and the predicate for all intents and purposes. In other words, it's a tautology (a circular argument) to define miracles as just those events that are explainable by undiscovered natural laws, for there's always room for the unknown to loom.

I urge you to read both Antony Flew's original parable and also his newest book, *There Is a God.* This legendary British philosopher and devout atheist garnered worldwide headlines when he turned theist. Perhaps it's just a coincidence that I thought of Flew in respect to my son's quantum jumps; perhaps it's something else, for Flew is also considered one of the world's leading authorities on miracles. You decide. What does it all mean? Does it need to mean anything at all?

❖❖❖ ❖❖❖

chapter 2

YOU'RE RIGHT WHERE YOU'RE SUPPOSED TO BE

*"Serendipity is looking in a haystack for a needle
and discovering a farmer's daughter."*
— Julius Comroe, Jr.

A popular notion nowadays flatly states: "You're exactly where you're supposed to be." That's an interesting idea. What does it mean?

Life-after-death research, typically examining past-life cases and near-death experiences, offers perhaps the best evidence of an individual essence (spirit, soul, your term of choice) as having a place of origin other than as a zygote (the early cell cluster before the embryo stage). It seems to support a destiny outside of becoming just another bit of landfill, eventually to share atoms with the bark of a tree, the scales of a fish, an outcropping of granite, and so forth.

If the afterlife research is to be believed, then each of us will experience both birth and death and perhaps rebirth. This scheme suggests a purpose or reason for life itself and, further, for what each of us is meant to do with our lives. *Okay,* you may be thinking, *so what's new? I've heard all this before.*

Doing and Knowing

I like to think of it this way: Say I use a computer to study pole-vaulting. I know the exact angle at which the pole must be set down relative to my height, weight, and speed; and I also know the velocity I must attain for maximum thrust. I know how many steps I must take, and so I know the point from which I should begin my approach. I've studied the position of the body throughout the jump, so I know when and where I should change my angle relative to the pole, where I want my body to be as I clear the bar, and so on. I've used advanced mathematics to do very precise calculations, and I've confirmed my knowledge by generating a computer simulation.

Does all of this mean that I can pole-vault? Do you think for one minute that anyone armed with all this "knowing" could simply go out for the first time and execute the action perfectly? No. Just because I understand the theoretical how doesn't mean I know the practical how.

I think of existence before our lives here-and-now—whatever else it may have been—to have been a state of consciousness. From that perspective, we all more or less know how and why we spend an incarnation or more on Earth, and I suggest that our purpose is as much to *do* with what we already *know* as it is anything else.

Doing and knowing aren't necessarily the same thing. Still, doing implies that this is a world of action, not inaction; of attention, not inattention; a world of purpose, not aimless wanderings, blind consumption, or an evolutionary arms race solely for the preservation of the species.

The phrase "exactly where I'm supposed to be" implies several things, none of which preclude the possibility of "getting the hell out of here." In other words, just because I'm in a certain place doesn't mean I'm supposed to remain there for any length of time, nor does it mean I'm to do nothing but accept that where I am is where I'm supposed to be.

The Face on the Wall

When I was six or seven years old, I sometimes saw a face appear on the wall as if to scare me or to share some unspoken truth. The face was stern. Its eyes were penetrating, its features were hard and sharp, and the neck was full and strong. The face never spoke, but it did frighten me. It appeared when I least expected it, and I never found any correlation between when and where it happened. As soon as it materialized, I vacated the room. Fortunately the face never came while I was in bed, although I experienced more than one terror-filled night, worrying that it would appear.

One day while I was visiting my grandmother in Lander, Wyoming, the face appeared out of nowhere on her living-room wall. I'd thought I was safe and had even looked forward to the visit because Wyoming wasn't my home state. Somehow I'd thought the face couldn't follow me there. (The thought patterns of childhood can be quite interesting upon later reflection.)

With strength and determination I didn't know was in me, I stopped, looked squarely at the face, and ordered it away: "Leave and do not return. You are not welcome! Begone now!" I then turned and left the room, and I've never seen the face since.

Why was it there? What was I supposed to do? Did I do the right thing? Should I have asked it a question? Was it where it was supposed to be? Was it real or was it a hallucination? If it was an illusion, it sure fooled me—not just then but still to this day.

Was I exactly where I was supposed to be, destined to be accompanied by a face for the rest of my life, or was it okay for me to order it away? And if it wasn't okay, am I now forever in the wrong place? But how could I ever be in the wrong place if I'm always in the right place? Doesn't the axiom say that we're always in the right place? Does the statement itself make any sense?

A Meeting with a Stranger

When I was a teenager in Utah, I left home one bright afternoon to cut a Christmas tree for my family. I'd driven up Butterfield Canyon when snow began to fall. It came down fast and heavy, and soon I found myself stuck just outside a small copper-mining town. I took refuge in a hotel for the night and phoned my parents. I told them of my predicament, and we decided that I'd try to get home again in the morning before my Father attempted to come get me.

There was no café or other eating establishment open, so I looked for what I could find in the lobby's vending machine, and that wasn't very much. An older gentleman noticed my hunger and offered me a sandwich and a Twinkie. I was grateful, so when he began talking to me about religion and the book he'd written entitled *The Only True Book between Man and God,* I listened.

I was a very religious young man and had earned several individual awards from my Mormon church. I was a Life Boy Scout, lacking only two merit badges for achieving the rank of Eagle. I'd been ordained at the age of 12 and in every way was an active, devout follower of my church. My father had stopped smoking by having elders from our faith lay their hands on him in prayer. I was well read in our spiritual texts, and so I didn't feel at all threatened when my host that evening began to speak of his book.

He'd been a member of my faith and, in his words, he'd left due to a direct revelation—thus, his book. We talked all night long. I countered much of what he said, only for him to rebut my points. He was well read in philosophical subjects I'd never heard of, or at least it certainly seemed so. By morning, I was uncertain about what I believed. He introduced me to many ideas and apparent facts that I later checked out. Most were accurate—perhaps all, for I was overwhelmed with information and in all probability went away leaving some of that information behind. The attacks he made weren't just on my faith, but on all of Christianity at times.

Once again, is this a matter of design? Was I meant to be in that place, to meet that person, to change the direction of my life? Or was it all a temptation that led me away from my purpose? If I'm always in the right place, at the right time, then I must conclude that I was supposed to be there. However, *why* I was supposed to be there is still open to conjecture.

Christ, Horus, Krishna, and More

I researched much of what I learned that night, and I found much more. If you aren't Christian, imagine that you are, and that Jesus is your savior. If you *are* Christian, this exercise will be both easier and more difficult, and the reason why will become clear as we go along. So as a Christian, you celebrate the birth of Jesus on December 25. You know that he had 12 apostles, Mary was his virgin mother, a star in the east guided three kings to his birthplace, he was a teacher at the age of 12, and he was baptized and began his mission at age 30. He performed miracles, such as walking on water, healing the sick, and turning water into wine. He's known by many names, including Lamb of God, Good Shepherd, Light of the World, and Son of God. He was crucified, lay in a tomb for three days, and was then resurrected.

Most people know all of these basic details, but did you also know that Jesus isn't alone when it comes to any of these claims? Indeed, a whole host of individuals have the same general history. There are some who suggest that Horus, the sun god of Egypt in 3000 B.C., battled the darkness of the world, personified as Set. The struggle between light and darkness (good and evil) took place daily as the sun lost to the darkness of night but won again in the morning. Horus was born on December 25 of a virgin mother (Isis), and a star in the east (Sirius) appeared to point the way to his birthplace so that three kings found it (three stars in Orion's belt appear to align on December 24). At the age of 12, he appeared as a teacher. He was baptized and began his mission at age 30. He performed miracles, such as healing the sick and walking on water. He had 12 disciples (constellations), and he's known by many names, including Lamb of God and Good Shepherd. He was betrayed for 20 pieces of gold, was crucified, lay dead for three days, and was resurrected. All of this was 3,000 years before Jesus Christ.

Then there's Mithra of Persia. In 1200 B.C., he was born to a virgin on December 25. He had 12 disciples, performed miracles, was dead for three days, and was resurrected. He's referred to as the Truth and the Light, and his sacred day of worship is Sunday.

Attis of Greece was born of a virgin on December 25 around 1200 B.C., was crucified, remained dead for three days, and was resurrected.

For that matter, take Krishna of India in 900 B.C. Once again, his virgin birth was signaled by a star in the east, he performed miracles, and was resurrected.

Dionysus of Greece in 500 B.C. was referred to as God's only begotten son, King of Kings, Alpha and Omega, and so forth. Here again is a virgin birth on December 25, miracles that include turning water into wine, and death followed by resurrection.

Indeed, a short list of religious teachers whose lives have included some or all of the aforementioned miracles include Zoroaster, Indra, Balai, Beddru, Buddha, Odin, and more. One might fairly ask: Why? The reason is based on astrological observations of the ancient civilizations. This more or less universal myth, or whatever you wish to call it, arises from the movement of the sun. The vernal equinox in the Mesopotamian valley was December 25. The days begin to grow longer, and so the rebirth of the sun was not only acknowledged but also worshiped. In fact, an ancient group known as the Cult of the Great Mother would sacrifice a bull on this day, cutting its throat over a pit and partaking of the sacrament (the flesh and blood of the sun) by way of the flesh and blood of the bull.

So, from the death of the sun for three days as it appears to stop in the constellation known as the Southern Cross (death on the cross or *crux*)—to the resurrection on the 25th, or rebirth as the days become longer; or from the virgin birth in the constellation Virgo (Latin for "virgin") to the celebration of light overcoming darkness during the spring equinox (corresponding with Easter), the myth shares its story based on agricultural societies' interpretation of astrological matters.

Questioning My Faith

I spent that entire winter night speaking with that stranger, and the next morning, with even more snow on the ground than the day before, I walked to my car. I started it to make certain the battery was still okay, but I really had no hope of driving home. Still, I put it in gear, and guess what? That Oldsmobile just rolled out of the snow, and I drove straight up out of the canyon and home as though the roads were dry. Did I have an appointment with destiny or what?

So imagine you're a young, devoted student of your religion, and suddenly doubt is cast over everything you hold sacred. What next? What did all of this mean? Of course, just because all of the so-called events of the myth are consistent with the story of Jesus, that doesn't necessarily mean there was no Jesus—but that's little comfort, at least initially upon learning of these historical facts.

For days—even years—I mused upon the thoughts of this stranger with his Twinkie, sandwich, and religious philosophy. I took some of the many questions that were uppermost in my mind to my seminary class. Although I'd been ordained, schooling would continue until I'd advanced to the highest priesthood level. I was informed that my questions were disruptive. I wasn't given answers; instead, I was flunked and asked not to come back. (The grade was later changed to reflect my actual scores, and I received an *A*).

Needless to say, I was left without religion. Did that make me agnostic? Not really, because somehow I still knew there was a God, although I felt betrayed. I discovered many others over the next few years who had similar feelings for different reasons. There were those who discovered inconsistencies in their faiths and accepted science as their religion, those who lost loved ones and felt God had abandoned them, those who saw evil in the world as evidence either for an uncaring deity or a dead one, and so forth. On and on, more and more, the people in my sphere seemed to be gravitating toward rejection of the classical anthropomorphic deity. By the time I was in my early 30s, I was surrounded by agnostics, atheists, and "in-betweeners," all living as though nothing but "going for the gusto" mattered. ("Go for the gusto" was a slogan on a TV ad back in the 1970s, which really had to do with living life to the fullest.)

Today I speak to many people who seem to be going through exactly this kind of shift. Where they end up will depend in part on their willingness to openly consider alternatives, including the error potentially inherent in the red-herring argument that conflates Jesus with the Egyptian myth of Horus. Whether or not the story of Horus was at some point in time, for some reason, superimposed on the life of Jesus wouldn't alter the value of his teachings in any way.

If you must believe in a magical story about the messenger in order to believe the message, perhaps you've missed the point altogether. Of course, if you believe that the message is about the messenger himself, rather than the information he brings, there's no flaw in the argument, for there's nothing unique about his story.

For me, life offered some proof that seemed to challenge my left-brain thinking. Once again, it's easy for me to look back and see a pattern, and therefore to assume that I was in the right place at the right time. Still, that could also easily be subject to further conjecture.

Meeting with Jesus

Several times in my life, a being whom I knew as Jesus appeared to me while I was meditating. I considered the idea that this was some form of wish fulfillment—it's nice, and it feels good, kind of like having Daddy at the end of the hall when you have a nightmare (an analogy attributed to philosopher John Wisdom). So I tended to discount these events, even though I never forgot them.

One day I shared one of these experiences with my son, who was questioning the "myth of Jesus" (I relay the full story of this experience in Chapter 19). Like me, he failed to give any credence to the notion that one should refrain from exploring the mysteries. I not only found myself describing my experience but also addressing the teachings of Jesus. Certain statements came out of my mouth that I've since verified: Jesus taught a way of life that was freeing to a people enslaved by the Romans. He failed to meet the messianic criteria of most Jews because he didn't militarily lead them from slavery, as they'd anticipated. However, according to the prophecy, the Messiah was to lead the Jews to freedom, and the message of Jesus did exactly that for those who listened—but the liberty was within as opposed to without.

The Teachings

A person's quintessential self, spirit, soul, or whatever you prefer to call it, was liberated by Jesus's teachings both here-and-now (the kingdom of heaven is here and within) and eternally. These teachings weren't new in the sense that they were totally original, for many were the inner secrets of the ordained few. What Jesus did in part was to infuriate the elite by sharing those messages with everyone. This riled the entire establishment and broke down their tight control over the masses.

Whether Jesus was the incarnation of God is something else again. My point is simply this: if he were only the genius of a man who brought a way of life that taught forgiveness and brotherly love ("these are all my brothers and sisters," and "whatever you do unto the least of my brethren you do unto me"), his life and teachings were and are remarkable and continue to be liberating. If we examine just the Gospels and take their teachings to heart, as with the beatitudes (blessings pronounced by Jesus primarily during the Sermon on the Mount as told in the book of Matthew), we find great peace, balance, and harmony within and without.

If we go a step further and assume that Jesus meant it when he said: "All that I do, you will do and more," then we recognize our internal "God intelligence" and the power or presence that is the "kingdom of heaven within." Suddenly all those things, from "peace that passeth understanding" to the mind-body miracles that medicine simply can't explain, gain possibility. This is remarkable in itself.

Now imagine that such a giant of a spiritual teacher died by

17

whatever means, probably prosecuted by the elite for heresy. What would happen? First there would be mourning, followed by eulogies. In time, the stories would become very exaggerated. Further down the time trail, as adherents shared more and more cultural identities, there would be additions, modifications, and bias added to the narrative. To make the tale even more palatable, myths would merge. At last, the scenario we see today, blending so many threads from around the world, would be the epic that's *the* story of the spiritual hero.

Today, for me, Jesus is real. Not in the sense that most people may believe, but in many ways even more present. For me, his teachings speak of true possibilities for all of us, for in his words, he's our brother, not our father; he's one of us. The "spirit of the law" as opposed to the "letter of the law" addresses the mystical meaning of creation, not the literal law of Leviticus.

I'm aware that all of this could just be my own rationalization. Still, intelligence tells me that myths seek to present a solution, and my experience synthesized by my intellect works for me. What that means is relative. What does it mean to you? Have you ever questioned this—truly examined all of it? If not, are you ready to do so now, or would you prefer to dedicate your life to something that you haven't given intelligent inquiry? Or am I just out to lunch?

I remind you that all of this began because of early experiences that seemed to lead me deeply into the faith to which I was born. Then the day came when what I'd been taught failed under the scrutiny of intelligent inquiry. Did that happen as it was supposed to? Would you say that I was in the right place at the right time? Or would you think that my brother, who never experienced the same stimuli and thus remained loyal to his religion—the same one I was born into—was in the right place at the right time? Or both? If both, then what does that say?

❖❖❖ ❖❖❖

chapter 3

ARGUMENTS OF EXPERIENCE

"He does not think there is anything the matter with
him because one of the things that is the
matter with him is that he does not think that
there is anything the matter with him therefore
we have to help him realize that, the fact that he does
not think there is anything the matter with him
is one of the things that is the matter with him . . ."
— from *Knots,* by **R. D. Laing**

Following my ejection from seminary and my resulting disdain for the adults who behaved so childishly—at least as seen through the eyes of a teenager, and with the advantage of some 20/20 hindsight—I must also admit to having felt discarded. I turned away from the goody-goody image many had held of me; and I chose instead to become an adventuresome teen with a fast car, cigarettes, and bottles of beer. I was angry, and like a wild animal caught in a trap, I was willing to chew off my own leg, metaphorically speaking. I began to resent authority of almost every kind and to distrust those I'd formerly looked up to and admired. My reactions weren't at all unusual. Young people everywhere can find themselves feeling betrayed over one thing or another and experience the emotions of abandonment that come when no one seems to understand or care.

Life is a great teacher. There are many forms of learning, formal and informal, but the one that's the most compelling comes down to experience. You can tell me something isn't hot, but if it burns me, I believe that more than I believe you. Such was the case with my view of God. Perhaps I was predisposed to interpret the events I experienced as being a meaningful metaphysical revelation, but then perhaps not. What does it all mean? You decide.

Psychometry

It's ironic, but it took looking into the so-called demonic side of things—including satanic cults, rituals, and the like—to open my eyes. I found myself working with various forms of parapsychology, including *psychometry* (which Webster defines as "divination of facts concerning an object or its owner through contact with or proximity to the object"). One day while visiting a local thrift store where I often found used books, I spied some new-looking volumes on the counter. I turned them over to see their titles and discovered that they were about the occult. I bought all of them.

I took the books home and entered my study with them. Upon close examination, I discovered writing in all of them. I decided to hold one and concentrate on whatever it had to show me. Suddenly, I was overwhelmed with images and feelings that were simply terrifying— horrible and not of this earth. Everything in my body said, *Get out of here.* Dropping the book, I fled from my own study, closing the door behind me.

For days following this event, I entered my study after work to feed my fish, only to find that the room held what felt like an evil presence. Then one day I noticed that the fish and plants in the aquarium were all dying. The room was also noticeably cooler than any other place in the house.

One day my brother came to visit. He was on leave from the Navy and had ridden his Harley up from California. He was a real gung-ho guy, so I challenged him to spend five minutes in my study alone with the lights off. Perhaps I suggested him into a special state of fear, for he lasted about one minute before running out, slamming the door behind him.

What had I done? What had I found? What did this mean?

A Different Perspective

The next weekend, I began my day with coffee and a book. I read until I was tired, then closed my eyes, took a nap, and dreamed. The dream was so alive that to this day I remember almost every detail. Evil came for me. Three main evil beings with a large entourage sought to take me to some destination that I knew was much worse than the frightening nature of those sent to collect me. In the dream, I laughed. I informed the beings that since there was such evil, there must be good. All things exist in opposition. I was relieved, for that meant there was a God.

After I woke up, I was amused by the experience, but it nevertheless held a part of me captive. It seemed silly to think that there was a necessary God, a supreme being, based only on a dream about evil. Still, I was prompted to review all of my experiences and ask again: *Do I have it wrong?*

Memories of psychic phenomena churned in me, and I began to rethink things, including the face on the wall. It still amazes me that I ignored so many events, took them for granted, or just plain thought of them as pure luck before that time. But there I was, revisiting my earliest childhood memories.

Playing Marbles

As a boy in kindergarten, I loved shooting marbles. I had a favorite taw (a shooting marble) that was my lucky one. One day at recess, I shot marbles with a few boys, winning all of theirs. When I was back in class, I examined my new collection—there were so many marbles that my pockets bulged. Then stark fear shot through me. Where was my lucky taw? I felt panicked, but I talked myself down, assuring myself that I'd find it when school ended.

When class was over, I went straight to the playground to search for my special marble. I looked and looked, to no avail, and then I heard—or, more accurately, sensed—a silent voice inside me say, *Close your eyes.* I obeyed. *Stand still,* it continued, *and just relax.* I tried to do so. The voice continued with instructions that went something like this: *Take ten steps straight forward and stop.* I obeyed. *Turn left now and go five steps forward.* Again, I followed the instructions. *Open your eyes and look at your feet.* I did so, and there was my marble hidden in the grass. How is that possible?

Faces, voices, and invisible hands? Reviewing these events as an adult, I remembered the train accident that left me so far from the site of the crash. My mother had suggested at the time that perhaps I was a walk-in, insisting that I'd changed. (A walk-in is thought to occur when the spirit of a being chooses to leave a body, and another spirit steps in.) At that time, I didn't even know what a walk-in was and—typical of me—I didn't ask my mother what she meant.

My Parents' Story

I also remembered my mother and father sharing an experience of theirs from World War II. My dad was in Africa, and my mother was in Idaho, staying with my father's family. My father's dog, a German shepherd called Queen, and my mother were sleeping in the same room. My mother was very worried about my father and had fallen asleep, telling him mentally that she loved him. Meanwhile, my father, in a foxhole in Africa, began to focus on my mother.

My mother recounted how Queen began to growl, then jumped down off the bed. My mother sat up, and there, standing by the bed, was my father. He told her that he was all right and that he'd write to her in the morning.

The next day, my mother wrote to my father and told him of the experience. He wrote to her on the same day, saying that he'd tried to communicate with her mind to mind that he was okay. The letters crossed in the mail—both had the same date. How is this possible?

Synthesis

A well-known statement that attempts to reconcile and explain the so-called unexplainable goes like this: first thesis, then antithesis, and finally synthesis. This triad of propositions is typically credited to the German philosopher Georg Hegel. The thesis is a statement/proposition that makes an assertion, and the antithesis directly opposes this proposition by stating its opposite. An example of a thesis might be something such as: "God is all good and the Creator of all that is," and the antithesis then might be: "There's evil in the world that God must then have created." A synthesis of these opposing intellectual propositions seeks to merge the ideas in one new proposition, such as: "In the beginning an all-good God created a perfect world, and that which we see as evil is either misunderstood by the human race or created by humans themselves."

So what's the synthesis for this conundrum? We began with a boy whose faith was broken by a chance encounter with a stranger, yet the same boy also had repeated experiences that would stir faith in the hearts of most people. Blind to the real value of these events, the boy saw only rejection. But it's fair to ask: Who did the rejecting?

A child doesn't always see things clearly, and as a young man I was no exception. I'd learned that the story of Jesus wasn't unique, and what's more, my entire notion of God was faulty. The divine was described as all powerful (omnipotent), all knowing (omniscient), all present (omnipresent), and all good (omnibenevolent). A terse review of this description by someone outside my faith quickly yielded shortcomings such as: If all is good, what about evil? And more to the point, can an all-powerful God build a stone so large that he can't lift it? This was nonsense, but it didn't seem that way to a child.

23

Broken faith meant at least two things. First, perhaps there was no God and no son of God—it was all a myth, a sort of sugarcoated neurotic crutch. Second, who could be trusted? These aren't unusual challenges for adolescents. Did you cope with anything similar? What does that suggest to you? Indeed, does it mean anything?

Still, with all that said, something beyond the "known" was part of my experience. What was that something? How could I reconcile my loss of faith with the realization that my experience argued otherwise? The synthesis didn't come easily or quickly—but in time I recognized that I felt betrayed by my definitions, my expectations, and other people, and not by divine forces or something beyond the known.

chapter 4

THE VOICES OF THE GODS

"We are all born with genius. It's like our fairy godmother. But what happens in life is that we stop listening to our inner voices, and we no longer have access to this extraordinary ability to create poetry."
— **Milton Glaser**

In the mid-1980s, I found myself near several channels. As you may know, a channel is someone who acts as a human conduit for information flowing from another, usually otherworldly, intelligent form. The entities being channeled are enlightened in some special way and offer advice to humans on how they can know enlightenment and even ascension. Sometimes the information channeled is scientific, such as some of the materials from Seth as channeled by Jane Roberts, or the ascended master Hilarion as brought to us by Elizabeth Clare Prophet. Indeed, there was no shortage then, nor is there now, of those who are channeling so-called enlightened beings.

JZ Knight

A number of channels have revealed rather remarkable information and abilities. Indeed, at least one—JZ Knight, who channels Ramtha—

has invited science to investigate the process. JZ is very pretty, slightly built, with beautiful flowing hair and an absolutely disarming smile—but that isn't what you get when Ramtha the warrior comes through. The voice changes and the demeanor becomes so strong that it's easy to get the impression JZ somehow just grew larger, taller, and definitely tougher. Not only do her walk and talk change, but so does the electromagnetic field around her, which some hard-nosed scientists discovered.[1]

Ramtha's message is clear, and although his understanding of science and history sometimes challenges orthodox views, to the best of my knowledge, where proof is available, Ramtha has been right. Take, for example, his claim that he was a Neanderthal, marched with an army, and spoke with his peers. Only relatively recently have scientists agreed that Neanderthals could speak at all, other than guttural grunts and sounds.

William Guillory

Another acquaintance of mine who channels is William A. Guillory, Ph.D. He likes to be called Bill, and he brings through several different discarnate entities. His typical regulars (sometimes he does report new beings), provide answers to many questions ranging from the political scene and events such as 9/11 to the most metaphysical foundations of spiritual practices.

It's important to understand something about Bill before I go on. He's the executive director of the Center for Creativity and Inquiry and the founder of Innovations International. He's a respected scientist; as well as an authority on diversity, empowerment, leadership, creativity, innovation, and quantum thinking. His most recent cutting-edge program explores the subject of work-life quality from a powerful new perspective. His newest book, *The Living Organization: Spirituality in the Workplace,* provides practical solutions for the balanced integration of work-life activities.[2]

Prior to founding Innovations International, Bill was a physical chemist of international renown, earning such distinctions as Alfred P. Sloan Fellow, Alexander von Humboldt Fellow at the University of Frankfurt, Ralph Metcalf Chair at Marquette University, and the Chancellor's Distinguished Lectureship at the University of California at Berkeley. Bill is a highly requested international keynote speaker and conference facilitator, with presentations in England, France, Germany, Japan, Switzerland, Poland, Mexico, Puerto Rico, Singapore, Hong Kong, mainland China, and the Middle East. He has facilitated diversity, leadership, and high-performance seminars for more than 300 companies, including Toyota, Dow Chemical, Eastman Kodak, Amgen, Hewlett-Packard, Brambles of Australia, Kellogg's, Proctor & Gamble, Merck, Disney, and many other Fortune 500 corporations. It's easy to see that Bill isn't your average person with an aluminum-foil beanie on his head.

I first met Bill soon after he'd resigned as chair of the chemistry department at the University of Utah and abandoned his pursuit of a Nobel Prize in favor of spiritual enlightenment. I was one of the first to read his book *The Guides,* which details his channeled transmissions.[3] Given his credentials, we'd expect Bill to possess a great knowledge of science, so when his channeled message is about that topic, we might just dismiss this as a form of alter ego, perhaps Carl Jung's trickster.[4] However, there's no reason to have the same prejudice in other areas, and those messages are equally original and brilliant. This means that the channel and his information aren't so easily dismissed.

Voices of the Gods

Since I had direct access to so many channels and they didn't all give the same advice, I became interested in interviewing them. First and foremost, were they making it up? Any of it? Second, did they apply it in their own lives, and how had their personal lives been affected by the experience? Since I was a licensed lie-detection examiner, I mused, *Why not give the channels lie-detection tests and then write a book?* I tentatively titled it *Voices of the Gods.*

Then two brothers in Utah, Ron and Dan Lafferty, swore in a court of law that God had given them instructions to kill. In June 1984, "two bearded men claiming to be prophets muscled their way into an American Fork [Utah] duplex thirsting for blood. When they left, their brother's wife and infant daughter lay dead, one on the kitchen floor, the other in her crib."[5]

The following description of the crime appeared in a retrospective article in the local paper:

> In March 1984, Ron recorded on a yellow legal pad what would come to be known as "the removal revelation." He later shared it with [his religious group], to the alarm of its members.
>
> "Thus saith the Lord unto my servants the prophets," Ron wrote. "It is my will and commandment that ye remove the following individuals in order that my work might go forward. For they have truly become obstacles in my path and I will not allow my work to be stopped. First thy brother's wife Brenda and her baby, then Chloe Low and then Richard Stowe. And it is my will that they be removed in rapid succession."
>
> On the afternoon of July 24, 1984, Ron, 42, and Dan, 36, set out to fulfill the revelation. In a battered green station wagon, they drove to the American Fork duplex of their brother and sister-in-law, carrying with them a sawed-off shotgun, a .30–30 Winchester, a .270 deer rifle, and two pearl-handled knives. They would use only the knives.[6]

This horrific crime was the result of direction from God? People I knew at the Utah State Prison informed me that these two brothers really believed that they acted on a divine command. When I asked a couple of channels about taking a lie-detection test and found that they weren't anxious to do so, I wondered, *Does it matter whether they truly believe everything or not?* I mean, just because they truly believe they're receiving messages from another world, another entity, doesn't make the message valid. I'm sorry, but if my God instructs killing, this would lead me to a *divorce* from faith. I simply do not see the Supreme Being as vengeful, angry, or expedient—or the murder of a woman and her infant as godly. No indeed, I can't think of anything less deserving of veneration or worship than a deity who orders acts of this kind.

Assumptions

What, then, should we think of channeled material? Is there a difference between the message and the messenger? Logicians recognize that the greatest lie begins with a simple truth. Just because *some* of what a messenger shares with us is both appealing and truthful doesn't necessarily mean that we should suspend our critical analysis of the rest of the information. In fact, many intelligent people have been led astray by just this sort of mental shortcut or heuristic (a tool for problem solving). A heuristic for remembering may be mnemonics, and one for handling the immense amount of information a human being encounters is generalization.

For example, imagine a small, soft-spoken man wearing a tweed sport coat, pressed pants, a thin tie, and glasses. Would you say this man is more likely a farmer or a librarian? Your answer would likely be librarian—not because the odds favor this answer, since there are many fewer male librarians in the country than farmers. No, your response is based on a mental heuristic that's essentially an averaged generalization shortcut. This device is summed up in the saying, "If it looks like a duck, walks like a duck, and quacks like a duck, it probably *is* a duck."

Not all well-dressed, soft-spoken men who wear glasses are what they appear, but we nevertheless make evaluations of this sort all of the time. In fact, we go even further. For instance, our implicit assumptions mean that we see a door in a certain way. Psychologist Charles Tart offers the example of a colleague being inside a restaurant that has an outdoor patio area. However, being unable to find a way out to the patio, he chooses to remain indoors; only to discover that the exit isn't a door that opens in and out but instead is a sliding glass door that he assumed was just a large window. Similarly, every one of us has categorized something and thereby become blind to an alternative way of viewing the object in a different context. Thus we come to the example of a scavenger hunter who's willing to pay thousands of dollars for a piece of wood measuring three feet by seven feet, only to be turned away because we don't have any such thing—and we close our three-by-seven-foot wooden door.

Think of the followers of David Koresh or those who believed in James Warren "Jim" Jones. Many of them were well-to-do, educated people, yet somehow their mental heuristics led them astray. Does that mean that we must be constantly vigilant, forever challenging our information intake?

I eventually decided that the idea of giving lie-detection examinations to channels was no more promising than the idea of doing push-ups on the ceiling. However, I've never viewed the information passed on by channels in the same way since that time. Perhaps it's possible to genuinely receive valuable information on one day and be dry the next, yet still have a need (for whatever reason) to meet expectations and therefore make up a transmission and its content. After all, even the greatest minds in history have stumbled while nevertheless leaving us with incredible insight. From Aristotle to Einstein, the world is both better off and aware that "men are mortal"—and that means they make mistakes.

Much of what many believe is based upon material provided by a trusted messenger. How much of the message really deserves our total confident trust? Just how many mental shortcuts frame our beliefs and thereby our expectations—and thus much of our reality? I don't think we throw out the message on the basis of the messenger, for the two aren't the same. Still, I don't think we wholly and uncritically accept any message regardless of the messenger either.

What do you think, and what does that mean?

chapter 5

MIRACLES

"The Ultimate Ground of Being is you."
— from *The Book on the Taboo Against Knowing Who You Are,*
by **Alan Watts**

Webster's first definition of the word *miracle* is "an extraordinary event manifesting divine intervention in human affairs." I've certainly experienced some interesting events and at least one true miracle in my own life. I've since learned that it's not uncommon for ordinary people to undergo extraordinary happenings.

In 1969, while living in Twin Falls, Idaho, I left the retail store I worked at to visit the warehouse. I drove across town, looking carefully in both directions as I crossed intersecting one-way streets. Each of these streets had a stop or yield sign. About halfway through one such set of crossroads, I noticed with my peripheral vision that an automobile was approaching on my left. I looked, and saw that the car was coming at me at a speed far greater than the 30-miles-per-hour speed limit. I stepped on the gas in an attempt to get out of the intersection, and the next thing I knew, my car was resting on a large tree and a fire hydrant. Someone yelled, "There's gas leaking!"

I had to jam my shoulder hard into the driver's side door more than once to get it open, but after I'd succeeded, I found I couldn't exit. I was tied to the seat of the car somehow. Baffled, I searched for the restraint and discovered that I was wearing a seat belt. At that time, I never wore seat belts—never!

But this device probably saved my life. I was in a 1968 Malibu Classic, and it was totaled. The car that hit me was estimated to be traveling well in excess of 100 miles per hour. My Chevy was thrown several feet into the air and across the street, but I survived without a scratch. The occupants of the other vehicle were stone drunk.

Not possible? Freak accident? Or had I put the seat belt on and then forgotten about it?

Miracles

I get a fair amount of feedback from my readers and customers, and I both enjoy and appreciate it. I've heard many miracle stories, a couple of which, with the writers' permission, I share with you.

Dear Eldon,

I could hardly believe my eyes when I turned on my computer this evening. I'd received a copy of InnerTalk about two months ago, but had misplaced it. Today I went on a hunt for it all over my house, when God told me where to look. (He always helps me find lost items.) I was looking for an audio on success that I could use with some middle-school students I'll teach this semester. I did a double take when I saw that I'd also received a copy of your online newsletter the same day.

If I may bore you for another minute, I'd like to tell you of our miracle last year. My college-age daughter had received her income-tax refund check in the mail. I was the one who walked down to the mailbox that day. After I went back up the driveway and into the house, I laid the mail on my desk. It occurred to *me that the brown tax-refund envelope wasn't in with the other letters. I said to myself, <u>It was with the other mail because I read the front of the envelope.</u> I looked all over my house as I retraced my steps. No brown envelope.*

When my daughter and her boyfriend arrived several hours later, they searched outside, in the street, and in the ditch alongside it. No brown envelope. I was devastated because it was my fault. We even had our next-door neighbor looking.

Two months later as I was getting out of my car, something told me to look in the direction of the basement window. All I saw was a crumpled-up old envelope. <u>My God,</u> I thought, <u>it's brown!</u> When I reached down and picked it up, I discovered that it was a tax-refund envelope, weather-beaten, crumpled, and stuck in the middle of my basement window with a faded (but still usable) $300 check inside. My daughter and I immediately said, "It's a miracle!"

Norma Bryant Howard
(yes, you may use my name)

Here's another:

After law school, I took the bar exam for my state. It was a three-day, all-day examination. The night before the final day of the test, I couldn't get to sleep, no matter what I tried. The longer I lay awake and realized the importance of getting a good night's rest, the more panicked and wakeful I became. This had only happened to me once before, and that was the night before my first exam in law school three years prior. I think I finally got to sleep around 5 A.M. and had to get up about 6:30.

Needless to say, I was exhausted the next day during the test. I trudged through the morning, and my thinking was slow and unclear. At lunch, I felt hopeless and didn't know how I'd make it through the afternoon session. I knew I'd humiliate myself, my family, and my school if I failed the bar, to say nothing of the gut-wrenching process of retaking the exam. I called my wife and asked her to pray for me. I also requested that she call her mother and grandmother, who were strong Christians, and ask them to pray for me, too. I prayed briefly during the lunch hour as well.

Something happened to me in the afternoon session. That part of the exam was multiple choice, and it seemed that I knew every answer. I recognized that I was tired and read each question carefully, but the response to each question was clear to me. When I reached my car after the exam, I prayed right there, thanking God for helping me so clearly and specifically.

I'd never had that experience in taking any test before. I didn't have a strong belief in God at that point in my life, but I knew something had happened to me that day, and it strengthened my belief in a higher power. It didn't make me start going to church more regularly, I don't think, although it should have. I don't think I quite knew what to do with the experience. I'm a very analytical person and not prone to being touchy-feely or acting on emotions. I tried to rationalize what had happened, but I couldn't get very far with it. I knew somehow that I couldn't explain away this experience. It has stayed with me always.

It was only years later that I finally came to accept Jesus Christ as my Savior. But it was that one event, together with a few other things, that was significant in bringing me to salvation and a real relationship with God.

H. D.

A colleague of mine has written a book titled *Incidents Beyond Coincidence,* in which nothing but miracles are retold.[1] There are stories about miracles from around the world and across all recorded times. Some may be explained in one way or another using a rational approach, but many simply can't be. Does a miracle qualify as evidence for something? If so, what?

The Value of Reason

Since this book is about the meaning of life, it's absolutely fair to talk about miracles. When I asked around, many people had miracles to share. Some assert that miracles are totally explainable and thus aren't actually miraculous. How can experience be so totally denied?

Reason has been held out by many, particularly those in academia, as the preferred method by which modern humankind should live. Reason definitely has its place, but it's only one aspect of our world experience. Our sense mechanisms are as important and, indeed, far superior in many instances. Factually, reason is often just 20/20 hindsight. That is, research shows clearly that often one may make a decision or carry out an action on the basis of consciously unknown stimuli. Both subliminal and split-brain studies have robust data showing how the mind will then make up a reason for the decision or action.[2] In other words, the mind needs to think it knows what and why it makes a certain choice, but at least from the perspective of the conscious mind, it often doesn't have a clue. That being the case, the superiority of reason can fairly be called into question.

Our Senses

Think about your other senses, including the possibility of those you no longer use or are aware of. My acquaintance Ingo Swann, in his book *Your Nostradamus Factor,* insists that all of us possess many psychic talents, including the ability to mimic his successes.[3] His experiments have made Swann well known in the intelligence community and at the Stanford Research Institute. So think of yourself as possibly having more than just the so-called five senses.

In *The Origin of Consciousness in the Breakdown of the Bicameral Mind,* Julian Jaynes, Ph.D., makes a compelling case for a time in history when our primary communication was telepathic. For Jaynes, the oracles of the past are potentially evidence for this method of information processing.[4] So when the hairs on the back of your neck stand up for some unknown reason, perhaps you're noticing some former method of communication—some older sense, if you will, that has been turned off by lack of use. Like a muscle that atrophies, this method of knowing your world is no longer available.

It's not hard to imagine a time when we may well turn off other senses in favor of our visual, auditory, or reasoning faculties—is it? I think not. If we're to know our world, however, I think using all of our senses is required. We feel many things. Sometimes we know things without understanding how.

I remember walking into a geometry class for the first time. I was in my teens and had never studied the subject, yet when I picked up the text and looked through it, I knew everything we were going to learn. There were some terms I needed to sound out, but all of the formulas, ideas, and so forth were somehow already in my memory banks. This blank slate, the tabula rasa of John Locke, wasn't so blank.[5] How is that possible?

Apollo 14 astronaut Edgar Mitchell reported conducting psychic experiments from space. More important, he shared some of his feelings while orbiting the Earth. From his feeling, his experience, and all that his formal education has taught him, he came to a level of knowing that led to establishing the Institute of Noetic Sciences. *Noetic* means knowing without the certainty of understanding how you do so. Is this reason as we usually think of it?

Grand Organizing Designer

My beautiful niece Sheena received a full scholarship to the University of Cambridge. She recently reviewed some of my video work and sent my wife this e-mail:

I spent some time going through a few of Uncle Eldon's videos, and then I came across the self-actualization one. I like the way he talks about putting your head on your pillow at night and knowing you made a difference. I suppose that explains quite nicely why you both do what you do—to make a difference. My favorite video was GOD Plays Hide and Seek. I like that, I agree, but only when GOD = Grand Organizing Designer. I'm not sure about the word designer as such; I might argue that there isn't necessarily any design but simply the results of lots of time for evolution—of the universe and of life. I wonder if things are the way they are for a reason, or just as a consequence of survival of the fittest. I can't even prove that I exist; this entire universe may just be a computer simulation and we might just think like this in order to power a bigger battery, outside of the cyber world. Who knows? [Emphasis added.]

This is an extremely bright young woman, and in the pursuit of pure logic, she has a point. Philosophers have argued these matters for millennia. René Descartes insisted that because he could doubt his existence, he must exist.[6] Immanuel Kant pointed out how ridiculous it would be to doubt one's existence while one's appendix ruptured.[7]

Who Am I?

Science understands the world by one of three approaches: materialism, reductionism, or randomness. The problem with these is that they eliminate purpose from the human condition, and this undermines not only our quality of life but also the whole of our social morality. If the human condition is only a matter of randomness existing in a material world absent any higher meaning, everything simply a reduction of parts, then the only significance life can have is survival at any cost. Somehow that pales when we look deep inside ourselves and find qualities such as altruism, sacrifice, love, and so forth. Life, after all, includes all of these things.

As wonderful as I think my niece is, what purpose does reason play if it fails to deal with real life? When a human being experiences life—be it pain, joy, laughter, love, awe, or anger—the emotion has a definite existential meaning. Not to belabor a long and drawn-out philosophical argument, but what does it mean to favor a rational process that leads nowhere? While it's intellectually stimulating to entertain these thoughts, the real value is the inquiring process that comes about as a result. The chief question remains: Who am I?

A broken love affair can make it seem as though the end of life is near—or should be. There's no rational reason for this based on logic alone. Yet for the millions who've lost a loved one, the experience can be absolutely overwhelming. Is this an invalid conduit of human experience? Is emotion unnecessary, or is it only some form of Darwinian mutation that serves a purpose appropriate to advancing the survivability of the species?

Living just in our heads isn't living at all. To be fully alive, we must integrate the subjective aspect of our own lives as well as those of others. To do this, it's necessary to recognize an entire level of experience that doesn't necessarily open itself to rational logic—or as Kant would say, pure reason. Indeed, using Kant's work, we could say that we must include practical reason, and therefore our experiences, real-life adventures, and feelings—all of that stuff that we experience. Miracles are experienced and witnessed every day by someone somewhere in the world. Acknowledging them is part of the true value of life. Denying all of our other feeling/knowing faculties is absurd, so balancing all, it would seem, is the middle path. Thesis, antithesis, and synthesis may well be our best mediators.

What do you think? What does it all mean, anyway?

chapter 6

PURPOSE

"You are your parents' donation to human evolution."
— from *The Roots of the Self* by **Robert Ornstein**

In 1986, the thoroughbred Ferdinand won the Kentucky Derby. He was later slaughtered for food. Winning the Derby wasn't sufficient to guarantee a noble end.

Horse breeders often speak of destiny. Great horses have a destiny just as tales of courage say that great men do. Was becoming food Ferdinand's fate or was it the Derby—or was it both and maybe something more? Do destiny and purpose even have true meaning outside the minds and hearts of humankind?

The Ego

A number of authors out there today, both well-known and obscure, argue for the abolition of the ego. What does that mean? Historically, the ego is the mediator between the id and the superego. The id would have us following our baser instincts, and the superego wants to assert itself in ways that would not only throttle back those instinctual appetites but would satisfy its need to be morally superior and otherwise perfect. A well-developed ego is balanced between the selfish and the perfectionistic extremes. It knows when and where to serve itself and when and where to serve others. In short, it knows who it is and has a strong sense of its individual nature—or a distinct sense of being.

Eckhart Tolle tells us in *A New Earth: Awakening to Your Life's Purpose* that purpose itself is illusory.[1] Perhaps that's my interpretation of his message, but the way he puts it isn't much better. Purpose, according to Tolle, has two parts: inner and outer. The inner purpose is just to be—be who you are, like the lilies of the field. Outer purpose has ego attached to it and is therefore subject to error. In other words, if I say my purpose in life is to serve others, my ego necessarily becomes involved, for I recognize the good I do. The warm-fuzzy feeling that I get when I put my head on my pillow at night because I know my life has made a difference to someone is an act of ego.

If the "reason" for my life (and please note that the word is in quotation marks) is to lose ego, to separate my being from action that involves ego, I not only have the paradox Tolle says exists here, but I also have a peculiar use of words. Jesus, whom Tolle cites often, knew who he was and what he had to do. In the garden before being arrested, Jesus asked for the burden to be lifted from him, but he knew his *purpose* and carried it out. Was that ego?

Purpose in Life

Knowing our purpose isn't necessarily a matter of ego in the ordinary sense of the word, or a distinct sense of being. Think of a few icons for a moment. The Dalai Lama certainly has a sense of self-identification (ego). Indeed, if we're to accept many of the stories in Tibetan Buddhism, he may be in his fifth or tenth incarnation. The point is that he believes he has lived before and has come back to serve again. There is clearly a distinct individual sense of being.

Mother Teresa definitely knew who she was and what she sought to accomplish. Her id and superego took a backseat to her desire to serve something greater, yet she knew at all times who she was. Her ego sought to serve God by serving his children. Still, there's definitely the presence of an individual sense of being here since she admitted to questioning her path regularly.

The great Buddha is said to have died as the result of eating bad food. The story is that a woman brought her very best of everything to a meal that she delivered to him. Knowing the food was bad, the great Buddha nevertheless chose to eat it rather than offend the woman. This sense of identity is no less than that of soldiers who throw themselves on grenades to save the lives of their comrades. There's a clear sense of self-identification or ego in both instances.

Jesus, scripture tells us, throws the merchants out of the temple. He doesn't politely ask them to leave; and contrary to what many might want to believe, according to all biblical accounts he's angered by their blasphemy. Again, there's a clear sense of ego operating here.

Tolle and others of his kind, it would seem, are intent on a special form of Buddhist nihilism. I'm using the word *nihilism* here as meaning that nothing in the mental world that identifies us as individuals—ergo, ego—has merit or basis. This is his philosophy of an enlightened metaphysical strategy.

Nihilism

Buddhism is a nontheistic religious philosophy that distinguishes itself from Hinduism in many ways, but with respect to our purposes in a very fundamental way. According to Hinduism, the life force of an individual continues after death more or less intact, at least when it comes to consciousness. This life force may reincarnate or transmigrate. In the Buddhist faith, this energy ceases to be uniquely individual when the soul is successful at living. It's the *purpose* of a good Buddhist to live a virtuous life, hold nature in reverence, and seek oneness—unity that's like the atoms of all things, and some of yours or mine may have been a part of an oak tree or a slab of granite or a dinosaur at one time. Liberation from individual distinction—oneness with all, with the universe—is exactly what our bodies become in the end. The adherents of Buddhism see the soul passing from one life to another until *anatman* (no-self) is realized. This is a very brief description, but it's accurate.

Nihilism is a philosophical position that asserts the idea that there are no absolute values or purpose. Indeed, according to Arthur Schopenhauer's version of nihilism, there's a strong possibility that the universe lacks intrinsic meaning.[2]

What I mean by a special sort of Buddhist nihilism could be contrasted with the "rugged individualism" of America's founding fathers or with the Ralph Waldo Emerson essay on self-reliance that I read as a child. Are we all truly ready to surrender our individual natures, together with our unique gifts and abilities, in an effort to merge as one drop of water in an ocean? While this might be an appealing metaphor, the fact of the matter is that this kind of immersion robs us of the very gifts from the Creator that set us apart as unique, and thereby deprives us of the opportunity to manifest those gifts to their fullest.

Where would the world be without the egos of the likes of Bach, van Gogh, Descartes, Newton, Tesla, and Beethoven? All of these and so many more who have been critical to the advancement of our world are individuals with monumental expectations of themselves and, one might say, egos. We might also consider what's involved for someone like Jerry Lewis to spend the years and years he has invested in his annual telethon raising money for "Jerry's Kids." He has run national Labor Day telethons for the Muscular Dystrophy Association for 43 years now, raising incredible amounts of money every year. Jerry Lewis has an enormous expectation of himself, and he leverages his full weight in obtaining assistance from other performers and notables in support of his worthy charity. We can't say that he's doing this for himself, but he's definitely aware of who he is and confident that he can make it happen. That's ego—not a bad thing, but nevertheless ego.

Surrendering Identity

There are many examples of ego or a strong sense of self-identification in our icons. Indeed, I challenge anyone to provide a real-world example of the sort of immersion argued for by Tolle or the fundamentalist Buddhists of the world. In fact, when we look for the wellspring for this dissolution of ego, we must go back to Hinduism. There, to escape *moksha,* or the wheel of rebirth, a person seeks the union of Atman (soul) with the the Brahman (absolute) to become the proverbial drop of water in the ocean—indistinguishable from the sea itself. Is that meant literally? Are we to believe that our purpose is to lose ourselves in favor of a sort of "no-self"?

To surrender identity, giving up self in every way, has some appeal. With that comes a sense of freedom—from fear, labor, responsibility, and more. Obviously, the whole notion of self-improvement or personal growth disappears. Reincarnation isn't necessary because there's no individual to reincarnate. Perhaps knowing personal existence is a moot point—for there is none.

Self-Responsibility

As I mentioned, I read Emerson's essay on self-reliance when I was a boy. *This is what I want. This is who I want to be,* were the thoughts I had as I finished the essay. Emerson's brand of self-reliance necessarily involves self-responsibility. In his words: "Nothing can bring you peace but yourself. Nothing can bring you peace but the triumph of principles."[3]

All of my adult life, I've taught the principles of forgiveness and self-responsibility. Implied in Emerson's view is the idea that there are standards that we must hold to. This presupposes an active awareness and involvement in our world.

If action is necessary, then deliberate action is preferable. It requires planning, setting goals or benchmarks, perhaps recruiting allies, and so much more—and this all involves interactions that require ego.

I therefore submit that ego isn't the problem. Ego is, after all, the mechanism that mitigates between the irrational id (base instincts or animal urges) and the authoritarian superego (the overbearing nature of social consciousness or morality) and finds the middle ground that gives rise to such things as marriage (the socially acceptable way to channel sexual urges). Indeed, the more we battle to control the ego, the more formidable it becomes. The monster ego gains strength when we deny it.

The Gift

Now think of this: Each one of us is created uniquely. We're special, and no two of us are the same. Each of us has different gifts and can be anything we want to be. Unlike the Hindus who carefully safeguard their caste system, it doesn't matter if we're born into the lowest of classes; we can still rise up and become President of the United States of America.

How do we reconcile this thinking with immersion theory and loss of identity? To many spiritually minded people, the process is the gift. That is, each of us has our own gifts, as in the story of the talents in the Bible, and what we do with them is what our life is measured by. Said another way, the meaning of life is in our purpose and the extent to which we manage to both recognize and accomplish that purpose.

A Self Without Ego

A healthy ego recognizes the real you. Without that, how on earth do you "just be," which Tolle suggests is your first purpose. Word games can be tricky, so think about this: Who are you? Do you need to know who you are in order to be who you are? When you're naturally yourself—are you different from when you aren't being you? How different? What would you be if you were stranded on an island alone for several months? How would you change? What fears would you discover?

Ego is just another word for *self*, but it designates the self that seeks to be accepted and loved. Is there a being who doesn't seek these things? Is there a better word? Does the "higher self" have an ego? If you say no, then you don't believe that the higher self exists, that it struggles with balancing pleasure/pain factors, or that it deals with ambition for some form of progression.

I love it when words trick us. What is a self without an ego? What does that mean? Certainly "being me" in the Tolle sense doesn't mean to exist as an animal does. If the lion is hungry and the lamb is near, then the lion eats. Is this what happens when there's no ego? No— because you must have an ego to deny the ego.

To me, being without ego can therefore mean one of two things. First, it can signify losing the part of you that mediates between your superego, which expects you to be perfect, and your id, which is your basic animal instinct. This is using the term *ego* according to the meaning it had when it was originally coined in psychology. Second, it can mean losing your identity because you're part of the whole anyway. This appears to be what many spiritual teachers urge you to do.

The first definition certainly doesn't sound as if it would lead to the best possible outcome, and in the second, I have to question the very purpose for life itself. Do we really receive this wonderful gift of life, with all of our unique gifts and abilities, just to deny it all? These questions bring to mind a wonderful saying that goes something like this: *Life is our gift from God; what we do with that life is our gift back to God.*

Reconciling the Inner and the Outer

Now, to be fair, Tolle does suggest that the inner and outer purposes can be reconciled. That's another interesting paradox, for in his words: "The negation of time in what you do also provides the link between your inner and outer purposes, between Being and doing. When you negate time [by living in the now], you negate the ego."[4]

Are you negating time—living in the now? Living fully in the present gives rise to the realization that "the now" is continuous, including living in the present tomorrow—or does it? Is this just semantics? Are we just playing word games? Tricky stuff, huh? What does it all mean?

We opened this chapter with the end of Kentucky Derby–winner Ferdinand's life. I awoke recently to the news that Tony Snow, former White House press secretary, had died. The general report was that at the age of 53, Tony had finally lost his battle with cancer. I happened to catch a Fox News commentator say something that I have declared many times. Megyn Kelly said, "Tony didn't lose to cancer. Everyone dies."

I exclaimed out loud, "Way to go! Say it again!"

Why do we think of death and dying as a contest with a winner and a loser? In that sense, we're all losers—it's just a matter of time. Life without purpose seems empty. Without love, it's lonely and perhaps just useless. Either the human species needs to invent God and purpose to find life bearable, or God makes humans in such a way as to constantly remind ourselves in some way that there's something more. This can occur biologically (as with the anatomical regions dedicated to deep religious experience),[5] emotionally (as with true altruistic acts of unconditional love), or simply through some unexplained event—the stuff that many call miracles.

The Kingdom of Heaven

Think again: What does it mean today when we say the kingdom of heaven is within and that we're a co-creative force capable of manifesting almost anything—and at the same time we argue for the abandonment of the ego? Are we attempting to manifest the absence of identity, or are we seeking to make a difference in the world by some positive, helpful act?

What does all of that mean to you? Is there some part of you that truly doubts a higher purpose in life? If so, why? Do you believe that ego is your enemy? If so, how does that square with the idea of self-esteem?

In the West, we tend to honor individuality and reward individual effort. Should we? Is taking pride in ourselves an extension of ego? Too much pride is said to go before a fall. Is there a difference between a healthy ego and a corrupt, selfish, egotistical, and self-centered one?

What does *ego* mean to you? If you give up everything, do you really think you've released your identity? How is your identity different from your ego? Can you have one and not possess the other, or is this all a matter of convoluted logic designed to introduce a special escape—one that you could call denial?

At the very least, thinking beings should be able to find some consistency in what they believe. Argue for a balanced, spiritually adjusted ego—fine. Work to eliminate the personal, selfish side of a maladjusted ego—great. Halt the instinct to Edge God Out (EGO) and view the divine as the God dwelling within all—wonderful. See and say *Namaste* to all—fantastic! But to see the sacred in everything includes seeing it in yourself, and that isn't nihilism.

chapter 7

FEAR

"We acquire the strength we have overcome."
— from *Considerations by the Way* by **Ralph Waldo Emerson**

One day while I meditated, this thought occurred (the internal voice spoke): *You are to go to the desert. You are to go alone. You are to take only what you can carry. You are to hike back into the desert where you will be alone.*

I knew nothing of deserts. I was raised in a valley in the Rocky Mountains. That terrain was familiar, for I'd hunted, fished, and camped in the mountains of Utah and Idaho, but the desert held no such history for me. There was fear attached to being alone in there for days without support, for I was also told to leave behind my wallet with identification, credit cards, and so forth. In other words, I was to cut my ties with the outside world and travel to the unfamiliar. No phones, no support mechanism—only me, myself, and I.

I shared this experience in detail in my book *Simple Things and Simple Thoughts,* as it was indeed a very important event in my life. During that trip, I had experiences that aren't easily explained, if they can be explained at all. For example, I lay on a rock at midday, sunbathing next to a large lizard, when I fell asleep and awakened hours later, according to the position of the sun. I should have been badly burned, but to my surprise I wasn't. I had closed my eyes while looking directly at the sun, imagined myself to be a beam of light joining the sun, sensed myself traveling like a sunbeam, and then had apparently fallen asleep.

Earlier during this same trip, I was walking while meditating on the feeling of the desert. I was working on merging my consciousness with the landscape when I noticed a snake crossing my path. It slithered by as I stepped over it, and only a few feet farther down the trail did I consciously recognize what had just happened. The snake had paid no attention to me. I remember wondering if those old stories were true about snakes biting the cavalry but not the Indians because the Indians weren't the enemy of the snakes.

The desert helped me face aloneness, which is often at the base of fear. There's pain, and then there is solitude. The conditions of being alone, abandoned, and unloved frequently lead to surrender—to death, to deep depression, to helplessness and hopelessness. Many would say that this kind of pain is much more torturous than physical anguish per se, but then, what does it mean to distinguish one agony from another?

The Human Need to Care

As humans, we recognize the need to be accepted and loved. We organize our societies around support for one another; we care about our children and the weak and the needy. We donate money and time to charities and feel great empathy for the loss of loved ones, whether through natural disasters or other tragedies. That's what being human is—at least in part—isn't it?

So does it come as a surprise when no one does anything to help a 78-year-old man who's struck in a hit-and-run accident, thrown over the hood of the vehicle, and dropped to the ground facedown in front of several spectators? The victim, Angel Torres, and his just-purchased milk, lay in the street unaided by onlookers while surveillance video chronicled the entire event. Indeed, the video showed "cars zooming past and bystanders staring at Torres from the sidewalk."[1] This incident occurred in June 2008.

Hartford, Connecticut, Police Chief Daryl Roberts saw the matter this way: "We no longer have a moral compass."[2]

Do we? Are we so afraid of being sued or mugged that we've abandoned our Good Samaritan values? Did we ever truly have them? What would you have done?

Help Out or Remain Uninvolved?

Years ago in Big Bear, California, I was delivering a Sunday sermon about the principle of service and its natural internal rewards. I told a story about an accident involving a small motorcycle that I came upon when I lived in Nevada. The rider was an older gentleman who I would see sitting outside his trailer early each morning as I passed on my way to the office. He always looked so relaxed and so at home, as though the traffic wasn't present.

On this particular day, however, he was distressed, injured, bleeding, and lying on the ground. Spectators were gathering around, but no one was helping this elderly gentleman. I stopped and went to him. I did what I could until the ambulance arrived.

Days later, I saw him again sitting outside his trailer as I passed, and he waved. Without thinking, I both smiled and felt tears swell behind my eyes. He was recovering, and that somehow made me feel better. Why? What does that mean?

The congregation in Big Bear gathered after the service to chat and have a few minutes of social interaction over coffee, tea, and sweets. Several members seriously asked about the wisdom of helping someone in this situation, ever aware of the legal ramifications that could arise. I respected their opinions then and still do, but I had to stop and provide whatever assistance I responsibly could. What's more, I believe from this and other experiences in my life that the times when we go to the aid of another define us as being moral human beings.

I remember hearing of a story about a young woman who was chased in the streets of New York approximately 30 years ago. She was finally tackled on the steps to her apartment house by the assailant, who beat and raped her while several witnesses looked on. None of *them* acted either. How could this happen? But then, that was long ago. Our society is more civilized today, isn't it?

The answer is both clear and offensive: no! Why not? Research tends to show that humans can easily be seduced into ignoring the most heinous of acts, but that's in the lab isn't it?[3] It wouldn't happen to trained people, would it?

The dateline is June 20, 2008, and the headline reads: "Woman Dies Ignored on Hospital Room Floor." The story is shocking: "Esmin Green, 49, had been waiting in the emergency room for nearly 24 hours when she toppled from her seat at 5:32 A.M. June 19, falling face-down on the floor." She died little more than an hour later, and she lay there without assistance from other patients waiting near her or, for that matter, from security guards and staff. "Green's collapse barely caused a ripple. Other patients waiting a few feet away didn't react. Security guards and a member of the hospital staff appeared to notice her prone body at least three times but made no visible attempt to see whether she needed help."[4]

The Greatest Fear

So, what does this mean about being human? Is there a moral compass? If there is, who has it? Is it possible that what you fear is what you become? Can you be in a crowd and still be alone? How do you think you would feel if such events happened to someone you loved?

The question *What does that mean?* exists because without our awareness, we've wandered far away from what things should signify. "Meaning" is much more than some definition. In fact, as novelist Henry Miller stated: "The moment one gives close attention to anything, even a blade of grass, it becomes a mysterious, awesome, indescribably magnified world in itself."

Meaning is more than just a mental construct. If being human means being a higher vertebrate animal operating in a Darwinian material world that arose as a result of randomness and that's it, a pure reductionistic perspective, then the world as Esmin Green and Angel Torres found it on their fateful days is quite ordinary and what everyone should expect. If that's not what you wish, then it makes sense to operate differently—or does it? What does it all mean to you?

Is there anything more fearful than to live without caring? Is there anything more terrifying than a life empty of meaning? Franklin D. Roosevelt once said, "The only thing we have to fear is fear itself." What are you afraid of—truly frightened of? What does that mean?

❖❖❖ ❖❖❖

chapter 8

COURAGE

*"Strength is granted to us all when we are
needed to serve great causes."*
— **Winston Churchill**

What is courage? Is it a selfless act that's offered for the benefit of others? Is there a higher form than this?

There are acts of bravery that are clearly in the name of self-preservation. There are true accounts of those who have freed themselves from traps by cutting limbs from their bodies. That takes the proverbial guts to accomplish, but what I want to examine transcends personal gain—the selfless courage that's offered on behalf of others. Where does this come from, and what is it?

If fear is largely about being abandoned, then perhaps the social side of that anxiety cultivates and perpetuates the idea of selfless courage. Perhaps it arises from some deeper sense or urge than socialization. Are we wired to admire and foster selflessness?

Movies portraying such courage move me in very emotional ways. In fact, I don't know anyone who, watching a well-acted film telling a story of selfless courage, isn't moved by the portrayal. Why is that? What does that mean?

Is it possible that selfless courage, expressed in an act that offers life or limb for others, is taught to us in the same way that we learn our other values? Do you think that extremist Muslims can watch a suicide bomber and find themselves as moved by this act of courage as an American viewing a fictional character saving the planet by sacrificing himself? Is courage a matter of cultural relevance?

Cultural Relevance

Some things seem universal, such as laughter, crying, and a parent who runs into a burning house to rescue a child. People going to the aid of others in natural disasters fall into this category as well. Is courage universal but guided by local morality? Apparently not all life everywhere is universally held to be sacred. How can that be?

In all parts of the world, children are taught something called ethnocentricity. This is the notion that they were born into the best country, have the best system of government, and so forth. Thus the notion of national loyalty is fostered. Young people are equally enculturated with a system of values that supports the social group into which they're born and raised. Religion plays its role and further deepens the "truth" of life. So in aggregate, individuals know little about who or what they might have been and believed if they'd been born somewhere else. Morality then becomes totally culture dependent—right?

Universal Values

Are there any values that *should* transcend all others and be universal? Obviously, preservation of life is one such moral imperative, for without it we'd be left with just the law of the jungle and the survival of the fittest. Our civilized world at least pretends to believe in the value of life or there would be no charges of crimes against humanity, nor would there be the charitable actions of governments when major tragedies hit other nations. Is this all just a matter of reciprocity? In other words, do I give you the right to life so that you'll do the same for me? Or is there truly a moral imperative that moves the human psyche to offer this right to everyone unilaterally?

One would think that religion and government, which are the tools society uses to teach values, would insist on basic, universal moral principles. What does it suggest when our institutions promote different standards? What does it mean when the life of someone who practices a particular religious faith is valued more than that of someone who doesn't? How can that be called holy?

Theories in penology (the study of prison management and the treatment of offenders) insist that at least one element underlying punishment is the need or right for society to exact a sort of revenge, to see justice carried out. Following from this, victims' families weigh in on death-penalty cases, and their needs (desires) are taken into consideration. This is a form of getting even—or "evener." Is it a healthy way for society to practice justice? Is this another form of differentiation between the relative values of comparable lives?

What if you learned that capital punishment didn't deter crime? What if you knew that it cost much more to execute criminals than to warehouse them in solitary confinement for life? What if you discovered that lifelong isolation was more of a deterrent than being put to death? What if it was revealed that a statistical error rate existed in death-penalty cases, showing that a certain number of innocent individuals were found guilty and their lives taken by society for crimes they didn't commit? At what point would you decide that capital punishment was inappropriate—or would you?

You may think that you share the moral imperative that all life is sacred until you reflect on your views regarding capital punishment, or perhaps you already oppose it and nothing has changed for you. How do you feel about the worst criminal you can bring to mind? Is there anything within you that would cause you to take up arms and use them with the intent to kill?

The Value of a Life

It seems that for all of us there's some mitigation regarding the relative value of life. A boat is sinking and only six out of eight people can survive. Two are old, in their 80s, and the rest are young (30 and younger). Whom do you save? Oh, but wait a minute—one of the older people is a genius with the answer to a significant world problem in his head, just waiting to arrive at his destination and present the material to the right people. One of the younger children is dying of cancer and has only a week or less to live. Now whom do you pick?

What if you're among the passengers, only one of whom *can't* be saved. The others are all fearful and willing to push and shove to be among the survivors. You have two small children and a spouse, and the other remaining passengers are all big burly men, none of whom will be left behind. What do you do? Is this courage?

Defining Courage

When we see courage, we know it—or do we? Does our culture teach this response? Is there an innate definition or root for courage per se? Does self-sacrifice count? If so, doesn't that mean that acts of altruism are also courageous? Indeed, wouldn't that mean that Mother Teresa's life was an act not just of charity and love, but of supreme courage?

If fear is all about pain or abandonment, is courage the opposite? Is it the absence of fear? We can easily see through this shallow question, for many so-called acts of valor have taken place in the midst of the hero's or heroine's deeply felt fear.

As we inquire into the nature of courage, it becomes evident that it isn't just some bold act, such as rushing into a burning building. In reality, it includes many softer versions, if you will. Sometimes an act of terrorism may be disguised as courage—or is this quality not a universal moral imperative? Does it have any natural root in the makeup of being human? What does that mean? Are there any values that aren't culture dependent, culturally trained, or quid pro quo in nature? What does that say about being human?

❖❖❖ ❖❖❖

chapter 9

FREE WILL

"Man was predestined to have free will."
— **Hal Lee Luyah**

Free will is an intrinsic human asset, or so some think. For others, it's an illusion, a notion that falls apart under close scrutiny in much the same way that values such as courage and the sanctity of life appear to be relative. If humanity is a matter of randomness interacting with some form of Darwinian direction, evolution, and mutation, then what sense does free will make? As purely a product of evolution, matters of the mind seem to be at least somewhat predetermined, don't they?

In other words, do you really think that a biological machine with the brainpower of Homo sapiens, the product of eons of evolution, would have been given rule over the mind and therefore nature? Of course, to say "given rule" implies intention on behalf of evolution and a sort of intention that goes beyond the notion of survival. Indeed, humans appear to be the most dangerous species for the planet, and therefore nature, that has ever evolved.

It's difficult to speak of nature, evolution, the laws of the universe, and the like and refrain from using words that can and often are anthropomorphized, such as *intention* or *purpose.* The meaning of evolution isn't a purpose at all. Rather, it's a fact of selection that tends toward the survival of the fittest, or so we've been told.

In a purposeless world, what do we mean by free will? The ability to choose the color of the automobile we buy? The chance to pick what we'll believe? The opportunity to determine our native tongue?

Choices and the Subconscious

Would it surprise you to learn that studies have repeatedly shown that your choices originate in your subconscious? That is, your subconscious tells you what you'll decide milliseconds before you consciously make the decision.[1] What's more, split-brain studies have shown that this disconnect is so complete that when you're asked the reason for your choice, you'll make up something that's totally fictitious. Apparently, the conscious mind must believe that it's in charge, and therefore it manufactures reasons for actions.

In classical split-brain studies, such as those carried out by Nobel laureate Roger Sperry and Michael Gazzaniga, subjects have had their brain hemispheres separated. A stimulus is presented to the visual field feeding one hemisphere, and then a task that's generally under the control of the opposite hemisphere is assigned. The subjects make decisions on the basis of information presented to one hemisphere that isn't known to the opposite half. For the average right-handed person, the left hemisphere is generally in charge of high-level decision making; it's the linear, logical brain. The right hemisphere is generally more spatially oriented and the area where subconscious activity seems to originate.

The language center in the left hemisphere gives responses according to its interpretation of the right hemisphere's actions. A patient can point to a picture based on what one eye has seen, but the left-hand side of the brain couldn't see; in this case, the person tries to explain their selection in accordance with the wrong input. For example, a picture of a snow-filled field is shown to a patient's nonverbal right hemisphere, and he selects a shovel from a list of pictures. But the left-hand side of the split brain doesn't know what input has been seen; it's unaware of the snowy scene.

When asked, the subject constructs a rational-sounding reason for choosing the shovel. When quizzed, he believes that this made-up reason is actually why he selected it. The most important philosophical issue is that the person doesn't realize that he's inventing a reason. This teaches us that our brain interprets our own behavior and gives us the illusion of a sovereign agency even when there is none.[2]

The Consciousness of Conscious

This finding suggests that "consciousness" isn't as conscious as we like to think. When we add to this the demonstrable fact that milliseconds before a conscious action takes place in the brain, activity in the subconscious directs what will occur, we rightfully begin to question what's meant by free will.

Benjamin Libet showed the world at least two significant findings: "that stimuli can register without consciousness and that conscious experience itself is a function of some additional system having its own properties."[3]

As such, what we're left with is a certain know-it-all left hemisphere that really *doesn't* know it at all. The fact is, this part of the brain seems to require an explanation for everything we do, and because it arguably doesn't have that information, it makes things up. It must interpret our actions and experience in order to provide coherence and make sense out of the world, including the inner world of the mind.[4]

The Genetics of Personality

Just as our minds don't function the way most people think they do, neither does our genetic code. Most think of genes as controlling eye color, height, predisposition for disease, and the like, but what about the genetic code that's linked to criminality and other behavioral characteristics? What about the sequences that lead to schizophrenia or multiple personalities? Where is free will when you discover that your genes may be behind your decision to lead a life of crime? Is that a choice at all?

Martin Seligman, past president of the American Psychological Association, puts it this way in his book *What You Can Change and What You Can't:* "This means there is a biological predisposition to commit crime (and get caught) . . . So crime, astonishingly, is hereditable . . . Most of human personality has a strong genetic component."[5]

Seligman states that this doesn't mean behavior is predetermined, just predisposed. He also points out that "even by most extreme estimates, at least half of personality is not inherited. This means that, at most, half of personality is fixed. The other half of personality comes from what you do and from what happens to you—and this opens the door for therapy and self-improvement."[6]

So if the mind is making choices without conscious awareness, and some of the choices are predisposed by genetic factors outside our control, then what does free will mean?

Mindlessness

Most of us would like to believe that free will is something we all possess for every choice we might encounter. In my books *Choices and Illusions* and *Mind Programming,* I expose just how much of our thoughts are already created by outside sources. It's as if we've been given a problem with multiple-choice solutions—perhaps *a, b,* and *c*—and the solutions offered are the only ones we can choose from. Very few of us come up with any additional ideas, even though careful thought would show options all the way from *d* to *z.*

In addition to this limited- or no-choice illusion, we're all subject to what has been called mindlessness. Simply stated, this is the absence of mindfulness, which is the process of attending diligently to our decisions as opposed to taking shortcuts. There are many mental time-savers we all use, and they're often necessary for us to get along on a day-to-day basis. Thus, we don't think about many things that have become automatic, such as signing our names; but we also often fail to evaluate our likes, dislikes, and actions on much more meaningful matters.

Ellen Langer, a brilliant psychologist at Harvard University, gives the following example, which I think illustrates not just our mindlessness with respect to likes and dislikes or beliefs, but also the absence of critical awareness of the many biases we hold for little or no reason.

Think of your favorite food for a moment; taste it a little in your imagination. Now think of the saliva in your mouth. Move it around in your mouth and think of how pleasant it is. Perhaps you can remember a time when your mouth was dry. Taste the saliva—it feels and tastes so good. Swallow the excess, as you've probably done millions of times before, and lick your lips. Now you appreciate your saliva perhaps just a little more than you did a few moments ago.

Now think of your saliva again. Imagine a clear drinking glass in front of you, and see yourself spitting the saliva into the glass. Now drink it.

If you're like everyone I've ever encountered (with only one exception!), you experienced a feeling of revulsion at the idea of drinking your own spit. Why? It's the same substance you rolled around in your mouth just seconds previously and enjoyed—so why?

Shortcuts, programming, genetics, unconscious processes— they're all illusions of choice. So once again: What is free will?

Free Will

Are we all predestined in some way or another to be who we are and do what we do? There are mystics with an answer to this problem. They assert that there's a plan for our lives that gives rise to the probability of certain things taking place. When karma is included in their metaphysical schemes, perhaps this means that an abuser in one life comes back to be abused in the next and thereby reconcile the karmic law by enduring consequences while also learning about suffering.

In order for this to occur, certain controlling factors must be in place. The stars, planets, and electromagnetic nature of the universe—together with genetic code, place of birth, parents, and more—are all elements that predispose the path but not the ultimate outcome. Indeed, even in the worst of karmic scenarios, the individual has the choice or free will to elevate his or her circumstances by various spiritual and unselfish means.

Is that possible? Are much of our lives about satisfying some preexisting plan? Is it really possible that the lemons will just appear and it will be up to us to make the lemonade?

At least one thing is certain in my mind: free will requires informed attention—our full and complete attention. *Informed* presupposes *information,* which means all the data we can obtain. Even then, is there ever enough information to make the best of all possible decisions? I think not. We can do our best, but even so we're limited, and that's just how it is. So what then is free will? Does it mean doing our best, given informed attention? Is it what you always thought it to be? If you discover that your choices have actually been given to you, do you conclude that it's your free will on display? What does that all mean?

✦✦✦ ✦✦✦

chapter 10

DOMINION

"You can have no dominion greater or less than that over yourself."
— **Leonardo da Vinci**

According to most people in our culture, and of course according to biblical tradition, humans were given dominion over the beasts of the field. I recently viewed a commercial made by People for the Ethical Treatment of Animals (PETA). A satire that compared a family of people with pets, its message was: sure, breed all you want, and we'll dispose of or perhaps keep and love the newborns, one way or another. Some found that message distasteful, whereas most just thought it was cute, at least according to PETA.

It's true that the future of animals is in the hands of humans. It's also true that domestic animals are destroyed by the thousands nearly every day. These are pets—cats, dogs, birds, and more. Obviously, this figure doesn't include farm animals, but then we're taught that such livestock are dumb beasts, so who keeps track?

Remember the 1986 Kentucky Derby winner, Ferdinand, who was later killed for food? Not even the fame of winning the Derby could save this once-fine animal. Americans have a romantic connection with horses, so the idea of Ferdinand being slaughtered and eaten is much more disgusting to us than it is to most members of other cultures. Indeed, there are places in the world where horse is a delicacy.

A good friend of mine in Utah once advertised to sell a small pony that had been his children's. A couple of Tongan men bought the animal. My friend and his children watched as the two men led the pony down the long driveway to the street where a car without a trailer was parked. One man grabbed the pony by the head while the other cut its throat right there in the street. It was barbecue time, and this fresh kill was dinner for their friends and family. Does that offend or disgust you? What if the children watching their pet being killed were your own?

Different cultures see things differently, and there's nothing new in that. Obviously, therefore, you may think PETA is stupid, just as there are some who refer to nature preservationists as tree-huggers. Then there are the sincere people who find these acts against animals and nature to be criminal or believe they should be criminal.

If animals *are* dumb, then there's still this question: Just because we can, does that mean we should? The reality is that the grain it takes to fatten a steer for the dinner table would feed more people than the animal itself, if we just compared the amounts of grain fed to people instead of to steers.

Now, in fairness, I must admit to having raised and killed cattle in the past while ranching. I must also admit to sending at least one horse to slaughter. I'm not a member of PETA nor am I a tree hugger, but we do have animals all wrong if we think they're dumb, and I know that from repeated firsthand experience.

Horse Sense

At one time I raised horses and owned an all-breed stallion station and racing stable. We stood (made available for breeding) a number of stallions, including several of mine. As a result, every year we handled hundreds of mares that belonged to other people. All of our breeding was done in hand, which means one person handles the stallion on a lead line while another one or two hold the mare. Each evening we would tease the mares (test them for readiness to receive the stallion) and breed. Sometimes, depending on the horses, the schedule, and other variables, we bred only after a daily palpation by the veterinarian. The point is that the horses were handled daily and with great care.

One day my foreman came to me about a customer who was delivering his mare for breeding. The horse didn't have the required health papers that I insisted on before animals entered our facility. I went out to meet the customer myself.

I saw the mare standing in front of the barn offices as I approached. She was a beautiful young animal, but obviously wormy—bony and with long, coarse hair. A very young filly was suckling her. After exchanging pleasantries, I told the owner that he'd have to come back when the mare hit her 30-day heat (he'd brought her in foal heat because the filly was only a few days old). In the meantime, he should worm the mare, give her inoculations, and get health papers for her.

The owner was quite upset about this inconvenience. He insisted that we should take the mare. I tried to explain to him that she wasn't in the best of health for breeding and that to protect his investment, he should worm her lightly with a paste wormer before tube worming her. Too good a kill of the worms could send an overload of dead parasites down her digestive tract, which is known to cause colic and kill horses.

The owner insisted that he'd made arrangements to bring the mare to us in foal heat and that he'd paid the stallion fee and therefore wanted her bred now. I refused, pointing out that the contract required the mare come to us with current health papers. The owner drove away angry.

He went straight to a vet who gladly tube wormed his horse, gave her shots, and hung health papers on her. This vet and I didn't see eye to eye, so I wasn't surprised to see his name on the documents when the owner returned with the mare and filly. We had no contractual choice at that point but to take the mare and do our best.

Two days later, she was in trouble. I received the phone call at home during dinner. She had colic that was discovered during early evening checks. As you may know, colic is an attack of acute abdominal pain localized in a hollow organ and often caused by spasms, obstruction, or twisting. It's the number one killer of horses. The intestines become twisted or tied in a knot, and the horse dies of peritonitis.

I instructed that our farm vet be phoned immediately, as well as the mare's owner, and that my employees keep the mare up and walking. I arrived at the ranch to find the vet already there. Soon thereafter, the owner arrived with his entire family, including seven or eight children. The night dragged on as my foreman and I took turns walking the horse. We did everything we could. She was given drugs to relax her and minimize the pain, and we'd oiled her stomach. When the vet left around 11:30 that night, we knew the odds were against saving her. She'd laid down and refused to get back up.

I went to the mare and took her lead line from my foreman. I sat down on the wood shavings that covered the indoor alleyway and arena where she was lying. I lifted her head to clear her eye of the shavings, and after brushing the eyelid and lashes clean, laid her head in my lap. She just looked at me as I gently stroked her head and neck.

Her foal was free in the passage not far from us. Some members of the owner's family were around the filly, talking to her and petting her, and the remaining people in the barn were standing near the entrance to our coffee lounge speaking to each other. For a moment the mare and I were alone, eye-to-eye, sharing only the helplessness of the moment.

The barn was full of horses. The alleyway separated the stalls on each side of the barn that was 303 feet long and 60 feet wide. The stalls on both sides were 12 feet square, and the horses in the 50-plus stalls were all turned away from the lights that lit the center of and entrance to the barn. It was midnight and well past their bedtime.

I stroked the mare and heard her filly neigh. As I saw her eye roll toward the filly, I thought of how sad she might feel if she were human, and I wondered if she felt that way. I spoke softly to her, reassuring her that I'd see the foal was taken care of. She looked at me, and the breath left her body. Still and dead, her head lay in my lap, and only I knew it, at least as far as the humans present were concerned. For just as her last breath left her, every one of the horses in the barn turned and came forward, leaning their heads over their stall doors into the alleyway. As though on cue, they all began neighing, whinnying, and otherwise setting up a vocal ruckus. Somehow, they knew.

My foreman asked, "What's wrong with the horses?" I told him simply that the mare had passed. I'll never forget that night. How could the horses know this mare died at exactly the moment she passed? She made no sound, and I made no announcement. How did this information reach them? What is there about animals that we don't know? How can we claim so much specialness for humans and know so little about other species? What does that mean? What does that say about being human?

I shared this story in my e-newsletter and discovered that it wasn't one of a kind. Readers shared both their views and some of their stories. Here's one:

Eldon,

We had a similar experience a few weeks ago. One of our horses developed a tumor on his head that didn't respond to surgery and treatment. It was encroaching into his mouth and airway, and we could tell he was uncomfortable, so we decided to have him put down. The other horses in another pasture were quiet until I watched our friend take his last sigh. A few seconds later, the other horses started running around, neighing. They seemed to know.

I think dogs do also. One of my female dogs loves babies; she even brought a live baby rabbit to me (the head peering out one side of her mouth and the tail bobbing out the other) and set it at my feet when the other dogs weren't paying attention. I put it under a trailer and when I checked a few minutes later, it was gone. I've seen her patiently stand over a wild kitten, almost seeming to talk to it for 15 minutes or more, and soon the kitten will be so attached to her that it will be a pest for her to deal with.

Best wishes,
Karla

Lady Balto and Her Ball

Not too long ago, my friend Lady Balto passed over. She was a beautiful German Shepherd I'd raised from the time she was five weeks old. We were very close and had many wonderful adventures together. I've had many great dogs, but she was the very closest to me ever. When her kidneys failed and I was faced with that final decision, it was the hardest choice I've ever made. I could only make it on the basis of the pain she was experiencing. We tried everything else first, including acupuncture. However, this story isn't about her passing but about her living.

Six years earlier, when she was five years old, she became very ill. The veterinarian had pretty well given up. I took her to an emergency facility, knowing that her regular vet didn't expect her to make it through the weekend. I stayed there with her late into the night. I talked to her despite the fact that she did not seem to recognize me. While talking, I began to see with my inner eye the games we'd enjoyed. She loved to play ball, so as I saw it in my mind, I spoke to her about being healthy again so that we could play ball.

Miraculously, she was well the next morning—completely well. As soon as we returned home, she went for a ball, and we played and played. A few years later I had triple bypass surgery. My youngest son was terrified that I wouldn't come home, so I promised him that I'd be back by the weekend. To keep my promise, I had to leave the hospital earlier than the doctors recommended, but I did just that.

A few days later, I was in a fair amount of pain and not in the best of mental states, depressed and ready to quit, when my friend Lady Balto brought her ball to me. She gently laid it down and nuzzled it over to me. Her big brown eyes were saying: "You'll be fine, and soon we'll be out playing ball." Tears still come to my eyes when I tell this story, for there's probably not much that could have lifted my spirits other than this act by Lady Balto. And she was right—as soon as I was up and about, we were out playing ball again.

Two Mutually Opposing Views

Numerous stories are readily available that recount how our animal friends have saved lives. The tales of animals' intelligence and their unconditional love and care for their human masters are in no short supply, yet we all too often seem to selectively ignore this and treat them in so many undignified ways. Why? Does this go back to our dominion over them? Cognitive dissonance means holding two mutually exclusive views. When we think of the animals that we love and those we eat, are we being dissonant?

Let me share another true story with you: When I had the stallion station, our daily collection of bad hay—hay that the horses wasted by throwing it out of their mangers, walking on it, and more—was enough to feed several cattle. As a result, I bought dairy bull calves from a farm nearby and fed them up for slaughter each fall. In case you're unfamiliar with the industry, dairy bull calves are typically sold soon after birth or killed immediately by being hit in the head. They're of little use to dairy farmers.

We tied off the calves' testicles and fed them the wasted hay. (It was actually very good for cows, as it was leafy alfalfa, protein-tested, and second cut, but dirty, so it could colic a horse.) A month or so before slaughter, we fed them grain to really fatten them. Each fall, my ranch hands, some of my friends, and I would share in the slaughter of those fattened calves. The resulting beef was among the most flavorful and tender any of us had ever eaten.

One year, a Jersey calf scoured. (Scouring is a form of diarrhea, and it can kill a young animal.) My ranch manager was gone, so I bottle-fed and cared for this calf. I dubbed him Boss, after Bossy, a traditional name for cows. Soon the calf was following me around like a puppy dog. He came when I called him, and he rubbed me with his head while I scratched his side and back. He was like an overgrown dog that mooed.

Fall came quickly, and it was time to kill the calves. Boss went with the others; after all, he was there for just that purpose. When it came time to load him into the stock trailer, my foreman called me to help. I told Boss to get in, and after I slapped his rear gently, he walked into the trailer. To make a long story short, this calf looked me in the eye before it was killed as if to ask, "What did I do wrong?"

Cognitive dissonance: I'd loved this calf, and I killed it for the freezer. I wasn't starving—not even close. The animal did nothing wrong, other than being born a Jersey bull calf. I ended up unable to eat any of the beef that year and, in fact, stopped eating meat altogether for this and other reasons.

Meat Free

As serendipity had it, I also participated in a study based on the readings of Edgar Cayce. The idea was to forgo eating meat for 30 days while maintaining a record of dreams and experiences. The underlying hypothesis was that the meat of an animal killed by modern methods was full of the fear and pain vibration that filled its flesh at the time it was killed. This energy was ingested when the meat was eaten. Thus we find our trigger points for anger, fear, and even depression figuratively filed as fine as the firing pin on a weapon; and the resulting hair trigger leaves us with much more negativity than if we hadn't ingested the meat.

I saw firsthand the difference in myself. Previously, I'd been opposed to vegetarianism. However, between the experience of Boss and that of the study, I found myself refraining from eating meat and growling at those ads that implied you weren't a real man if you didn't eat beef.

Today, I know that there are times and places for the ingestion of meat. There are cultures and people that depend on it and couldn't survive without it, such as some Eskimo and Sami peoples. My wife, a dedicated vegetarian when I met her, found herself craving chicken while she was pregnant with our oldest son. She broke down and had the chicken I prepared and ate with her. While she carried our second son, she craved beef. She didn't understand the cravings because she had only had beef once or twice before becoming a vegetarian and had never liked it.

She refused to eat the beef, and soon after our younger son was born, she found herself diagnosed with rheumatoid arthritis. The health-care professionals sentenced her to a life of limited activity and daily medication. She refused to accept this prognosis and used several alternative methods of healing, including consuming a beef extract, and today she's healthy and well in every way—free for years from arthritis. Ironic, huh?

Fido and Chief

What does this all mean? Do we get such messages so mixed up at times that we're uncertain about what they mean? Do many of us hear that our hard positions in either extreme are wrong? What do you think? Are there more shades of gray?

Perhaps things aren't always black or white. When I was a boy, I wanted a dog. One day, a stray German Shepherd puppy followed me home and adopted me, going everywhere with me. It wasn't mine, though, and my father advertised it in the local paper as a "found dog." Soon the rightful owner came to claim the puppy, and I regretfully said good-bye. Seeing my sadness, my father offered to get me a dog. For weeks, I watched the paper for notices of puppies that were within the budget my dad had given me. When at last I found an ad listing the right price, I was very excited.

That evening, the entire family went to see the advertised puppies. We selected one, and I named him Chief. He was half boxer and half German Shepherd, and he looked like a purebred Rhodesian Ridgeback (although I didn't know that at the time). Soon Chief and I were inseparable.

One day when I walked into our utility room, my father's dog, Fido, was there eating. My dad had raised Fido. This dog's mother was Queen, the pet who had slept alongside my mother the night my father appeared to her while he was actually in Africa. Queen had taught to me walk, or so my mother claimed. Apparently, when I was an infant, I grabbed hold of Queen and stood, and she walked slowly, forcing me to walk with her, or at least take steps. Queen's son Fido was about ten years old at the time of this story, and he was with my father whenever Dad was home.

Chief started toward Fido's food, and Fido went after him. I tried to stop the matter by putting myself between the dogs. I was bitten— not seriously, but bitten nonetheless—by Fido.

My mother told my father what had happened when he got home from work. The next day, without a word, Dad took Fido to the vet and had him put down. Even today, I feel both tremendous guilt over the matter and deep sorrow for my dad. I can't imagine how difficult that must have been for him. I've tried to imagine what I'd do if such a thing happened with my sons, and I hope that I could do the right thing.

What *is* the right thing? Could the two dogs just have been separated, or are thoughts of that nature just so much Disney-like fantasy where children's safety is concerned?

The Language of Animals

As a scientist, I'm aware that animals have their own language. Indeed, some animals, such as the rhesus monkey, have been taught to sign rather large English vocabularies. It's easy to relegate something, some life-form, to lesser status if it's unable to communicate. In the original movie *Planet of the Apes,* only when Charlton Heston speaks (writes in the sand) is he taken seriously, as something more than an animal used for the convenience of the apes. Is it fair in our modern society to ask: Who is the ape? Similarly, think back to the classic book *Animal Farm.* Ask yourself who the real pig might be.

We share our planet with many life-forms, races, nationalities, flora, and fauna—all in delicate balance. Intuitively, I believe that Edgar Cayce had it right: The vibrations of what we eat become our own. Everything in our universe differs only at the rate at which each part vibrates. Quantum physics makes it inescapably evident that nothing is ever lost, moving from matter to energy to matter, from entropy to energetic higher orders, and so on. In that oneness, we become our thoughts and consume accordingly, living or being what we've fed ourselves. Seeing this and seeking peace, balance, and harmony are easy in words, but what about all the gray areas—all of the "What does that mean?"

chapter 11

ANTS

*"Turn on the prudent ant thy heedful eyes. Observe her
labors, sluggard, and be wise."*
— Samuel Johnson

I recently had the pleasure of joining thousands at the Hay House I
Can Do It® conference in Tampa Bay, Florida. It never ceases to amaze
me just how much there is to learn. I had the opportunity to share my
work, research, and thoughts and to be informed by others during the
process, but an unexpected conversation led to a remarkable insight
for me.

Years ago, when I was a mere eight or nine years old, I spent several
consecutive days burning ants in my backyard. It's embarrassing to
think about it now, but at the time I missed the meaning of what I was
doing. I dug up large anthills—and we had many—shot some lighter
fluid on the area, and lit a rolled sheet of waxed paper that I used as a
torch to spread the fire. Sometimes I placed small milk cartons on the
hills and pretended they were houses going up in flames.

My friends did similar things to pass the summer days, so I didn't
think what I was doing was anything other than normal. "So what?"
I would have responded to anyone challenging me. Then one night

79

I had a dream in which the ant leaders came to speak with me. They were very courteous and formal, like grown-ups, and they showed me the devastation I was bringing to their families. I'd wrecked their homes and tortured family members, and they'd dragged back to their graveyards the burnt and twisted remains of brothers and sisters. They also showed me around their homes as they were before I'd started burning them and otherwise tormenting these creatures. In the days before my boredom led to this pastime, the ants lived in harmony. They worked together to build, encouraging each other to do a good job so as to create a strong future for the next generation. Their strength, courage, and work ethic were most impressive, even to a child like myself.

I awoke from the dream frightened and nauseated. I felt terrible for what I'd done. I never burned another anthill or ant. I abandoned this afternoon hobby for good, and in time thought very little about ants. Although with 20/20 hindsight I can see that my learning should have transferred from ants to all animals, it didn't happen quite that way for me. It did work well enough for me to refuse to take biology in high school because I objected to cutting up frogs, but by the time I entered adulthood, most of the message had seriously dimmed.

Praying Ants

Then one day, while I was riding in a limo to the airport in Tampa Bay, Florida, the driver and I had a conversation. It started with the nature of spirituality and the distinction between spirituality and religion. After some lofty and elegant philosophies, the driver looked at me and said, "You know what? I believe in prayer." He then went on to explain why. It was the ants again—ants that he'd seen in a nature show on television. Ants that he said buried their dead and prayed. "If ants pray," he told me when we parted, "then there must be a reason that goes beyond what we know."

As soon as I returned home, I checked out the information. Sure enough, in real life, ants lived up to my dream. I pulled a quick article off the Web from Encyclopedia Bugtannica, which began: "They plant gardens, herd and milk bugs such as aphids, raise armies for battles, take slaves, and even bury their dead in ant cemeteries." The article, titled merely "Ants," went on to speak of the loyalty, efficiency, diligence, sacrifice, and teamwork that ants share.

I thought of the many times I'd looked out the window of an airplane, down on the anthills of humans. Tiny vehicles traveling along skinny roadways, small houses and other buildings crowded together, itsy-bitsy people, and even more minuscule animals such as dogs carrying out their day—all just like ants, busy little ants with no apparent purpose to the observer flying by in an airplane. Yet on the ground, we learn the purpose of those little specks, their dreams, goals, ambitions, and more. I wondered what more I could learn if I lived with the ants.

How foolish it is for us so-called enlightened human beings to think that we're the only intelligent and moral creatures on this planet. How will we ever come to understand ourselves if we overlook the world we live in? Just where is the divide between knowledge of ourselves and knowledge of the world we participate in? How could a solitary ant gain personal insight without standing back and witnessing the entire ant world? It's all too easy to be so busy that we fail to take stock of the everyday things that surround us—or is it just me? Do you notice the lives of all the creatures large and small that dwell with and near you? Do they matter? Do you think there's a lesson from the ants we all could learn—and if so, what is it? What does it all mean, anyway?

❖❖❖   ❖❖❖

chapter 12

PSYCHIC SPIRITUALITY

"If it's the Psychic Network, why do they need a phone number?"
— **Robin Williams**

Years ago, a very popular and famous psychic channel (a channel is someone who, in an altered state of consciousness, communicates information from an entity from another time or space) contacted my office. He had an investment opportunity, and he wanted me to investigate certain people and their offerings before he put any money into the venture. He informed me that he couldn't ask the entity he was channeling for help because a profit motive was involved. I remember thinking, *I like this man, but this seems to be a very convenient story.* What's the relationship between channeling and other psychic abilities and spirituality?

In my opinion, the laying on of hands for healing is both a psychic and a spiritual matter. I remember my father having the church elders give him a blessing to assist him in his effort to stop smoking. They did this by laying their hands on his head and praying, providing just such a blessing. He stopped smoking.

A young woman I knew was told that surgery was required to remove a large growth near her ovaries. Of course, she was very worried that the growth was cancerous. She knew that I'd just become an ordained minister and asked me to provide a blessing for her medical condition. I was reluctant to do so, seriously doubting my ability and worthiness, but I can still remember the heat that flowed through my entire body, the sweat that broke on my brow, and the tingling in my hands and fingers during the blessing.

The surgery was successful, and as synchronicity had it, after the surgery her tumor was used during a medical specialists' convention that was being held in the city that next weekend. The growth was unique: it had imploded just before surgery. What does that mean?

When I was younger, I was fixated on psychic this and that. I had to experiment with most of it. One day while I was concentrating on stopping a pendulum clock, it did stop. I restarted the clock, tried again, and again it stopped. I told a friend about this. She and I tried concentrating together on the same task, and that time the pendulum ceased moving so suddenly that it was as if someone had put a hand in its path. To this day, I think she managed that result, but she gave credit to me. After a while, I sold the clock. Later I purchased another and tried to stop it, but nothing happened. What does that mean?

When Was My Time?

When I was teenager, I was told by a male visitor—an apparition, if you will—that something had gone wrong and I was to leave (die) two nights hence in my sleep. No way! I spoke out against this, and the next night three visitors informed me that it was the best course of action. Still I insisted: No way!

I never asked why, but I should have. I just decided that no one was going to tell me it was time to die. I stayed up all night on the appointed evening. Obviously, I didn't pass on. Not long afterward, I was in the train accident that should have killed me. What happened? What does this mean?

Life is a tapestry of events, thoughts, feelings, insights, and emotions. Did I imagine the visitors and the death message, or was my will strong enough to protect me not only on the appointed evening but also later when the train of more than 100 cars slammed into my Oldsmobile?

One night I was awakened from a sound sleep by the feeling that I'd been told: "Get out of here now!" The urgency of the impression was so total and complete that I arose, awakened my wife, and we left our motel room around 2:30 A.M. The radio the next day told of a shooting that had taken place where we were staying. Was the warning a lifesaving premonition?

Psychic Investigations

As an investigator and lie-detection examiner, I often used psychics. More than one case was worked out with their aid. Sometimes they were wrong, yet still right. I remember one such occasion when I took a psychic to a crime scene. The victim's truck had been parked under a viaduct alongside the main highway. Blood was spattered on the driver's side, and from initial appearances one would conclude that someone in the passenger's seat of the pickup had shot the victim. The weapon was a shotgun.

The psychic I'd brought to the scene was quiet for a long time, her eyes closed, and then she announced that two men with a sawed-off shotgun had been parked near the vehicle in a black truck. She gave a partial license-plate number, and soon I was confronting two men who possessed an illegal sawed-off shotgun. As it turned out, however, they had nothing to do with the crime I was investigating. They'd parked there, but not on the day in question. What kind of impression did this psychic detect, and how was it stored by the universe—or was this just a coincidence?

Odds on the coincidence theory are astronomical but not impossible. For some, there is such an effort to debunk anything of the so-called paranormal that it is safer for them to invent or invest in ideas that are simply absurd. If statistics say something isn't likely, why not accept that instead of insisting that anything is possible? *Is* anything possible?

A Cosmic Accident

Scientists often describe the universe as the result of some cosmic accident, despite the almost absolute improbability of that being the case. They go even further than that if you consider consciousness as having a role in creation. The uncertainty principle clearly shows that an act of consciousness—observation—is required to fix a condition, say a waveform or particle. To avoid having consciousness play an active role in this process, the all-possible-universes or many-worlds theory was devised. It asserts that at any moment prior to observation, all possibilities exist. Upon actual observation, multiple universes are created, generating simultaneous worlds and versions of you and me that exist parallel to us but according to different choices or possibilities that result from the act of observation.

The eminent scientist Bernard Haisch puts it this way in his book *The God Theory:*

> One tiny atom's quantum behavior replicates the entire universe and defines each alternative by all the possible consequences of that behavior. But at any moment, within each human body, there are on the order of a billion times a billion atoms, each making quantum transitions. In the Many Worlds interpretation of quantum mechanics, every human being, therefore, creates a billion times a billion times a billion alternative universes every second. Multiply that by the billions of humans on the planet. . . .
>
> In this view, there are a virtually incalculable number of duplicates of every human being springing into existence every second, each living in its own parallel universe, and each just as real as you and or I. . . .
>
> To put it bluntly, some scientists are willing to "create" a veritably infinite number of alternate universes to avoid admitting that consciousness plays a role in the operation of our universe.[1]

How the Universe Works

Somehow I *know,* just as I knew geometry without ever studying it, how this universe works—at least from the standpoint of God and creation. That may well sound like the claim of a madman, but in my life I've witnessed much of what I know move from the unknown or the farthest reaches of mysticism to the known or the world of modern science. Let me share with you what I understand.

Consciousness is not only not a local event but a universal one, like the ocean waves that are unseen many miles from shore bringing pressure to bear on those just reaching the shore. Consciousness, or the mind, has universal *epiphenomenon* effects (according to Webster's dictionary, "a secondary mental phenomenon that is caused by and accompanies a physical phenomenon but has no causal influence itself"). Consciousness is a creative force that for all intents and purposes is absolutely necessary to a unified-field theory.

Individual minds operate much like a transceiver, sending and receiving information. Think of them as special radio stations capable of getting transmissions and sending them. Many people keep their stereos tuned to stations that broadcast fear, limitation, shortages, pestilence, and the like. Others are tuned to angry, "getting-even" programs. There are many stations, and among them are those that broadcast peaceful, creative, and responsible programs. Our thoughts are largely based on the place where we keep our radio station tuned. Because our behavior is such that we seek out others who share our beliefs—as the saying goes, "birds of a feather flock together"—we share broadcasts with the like-minded and thereby reinforce our expectations.

Thinking is destiny, and thoughts are things. What you truly believe, you're likely to manifest or experience. More than just a self-fulfilling prophecy or a Pygmalion effect, it's really an issue of mind entering matter, or consciousness causing a waveform to express itself in our manifest world.

I began this brief section by saying: "Somehow I knew, just as I knew geometry without ever studying it," and now I ask you, what does that mean? Is this sort of information stored in a different location than the data accessed by the psychic in locating a sawed-off shotgun?

The Zero-Point Field

There are those who point to a physical explanation for so-called anomalies of information accessed by individuals and groups. The explanation is the theory that this zero-point field holds all information, including data that governs the physical (the laws of science) and that records all human activity (the Akashic Record). It's tempting to grasp this explanation and shake it in the face of nonbelievers as another piece of evidence for a spiritual reality, such as the mystics have described for eons.

The problem in doing so is at least two-fold. First, jumping onto any new bandwagon without thorough evaluation is never advisable. Second, does this zero-point field exist everywhere in all the universe? Is there only one such field? If not, what would that mean?

It would be very convenient to think of one zero-point field where both awake and unawake consciousness hangs out, along with the source of inspiration, the mechanic behind synchronicity, and so forth. When I was studying the Kabbalah years ago, my life was so full of varied endeavors that one evening I went to bed and silently posed the question: *Should I keep dedicating time to learning the Kabbalah?* As I drifted off to sleep, I was startled by a loud noise. I opened my eyes, and there before me, floating above the bed, was the Sephiroth (Tree of Life). I took that to be an affirmative answer to my question. The zero-point field offers an explanation for such a phenomenon.

Accessing the Field

I've always held that one mind can influence others. I believed this so strongly that when I was a young man with testosterone raging through my veins, I tested out the degree of this influence. In college, my anthropology professor was young and beautiful. I therefore concentrated during her lectures on causing her to scratch herself in compromising places. She usually obliged.

Sometime later, I needed funding to turn a hobby of mine into a business. As I went to sleep each night for more than a week, I visualized the closing table and the funds being released to me. It happened just as I had seen. I later regretted making this happen (if indeed I did cause it), because what I didn't do was visualize anything beyond the acquisition of the money. Take my advice: include success of the business in your visualization.

Is it necessary to have a zero-point field to explain these kind of events? I think not. Our transceiver model allows for mind-to-mind communication. Yet the notion of a collective unconscious as advanced by the brilliant psychologist Carl Jung,[2] or the idea of a morphenogenetic field, as hypothesized by the outstanding biologist Rupert Sheldrake,[3] do fit comfortably within a zero-point field.

My experience suggests that the simple linear models science often uses to explain life, the universe, and the mysteries of consciousness are simplistic and false. What does your experience suggest? What does that mean?

chapter 13

COINCIDENCE

*"Life is not merely a series of meaningless accidents
or coincidences, but rather, it's a tapestry of events
that culminate in an exquisite sublime plan."*
— from the movie *Serendipity*

Earlier I mentioned the marvelous book *Incidents Beyond Coincidence.*
Its title raises a valid point: When is an unexplained incident merely a
coincidence and when is it something more meaningful—or is it ever?

I think of my life's experiences and ask, *Is there another explanation
for these events that in aggregate speak of otherworldly matters?* Was
there something about the train wreck that I missed, something that's
a matter of coincidence? Had I seen a television commercial about the
safety of seat belts and somehow unconsciously buckled up on that
day in Twin Falls, Idaho, when my new 1968 Malibu was slammed
broadside by a speeding car, thrown up into a tree, and then fell down
to rest precariously on a fire hydrant? Could that be the explanation
behind why I had the seat belt fastened? Was it only coincidence that I
followed those instructions in my head that led me to my favorite taw
so that when I opened my eyes the marble lay at my feet?

Some say there's no such thing as coincidence. These same people are equally certain there are no accidents. If this is the case, then how can something go wrong? I was told that something had gone wrong and therefore it was time for me to leave this planet—to die. I refused to accept that verdict, but does that explain how things might go wrong? Is it possible that accidents are acts chosen to occur by the parties involved—or for that matter, by others?

Roots of Coincidence

Let's assume for a moment that there are coincidences. In a book entitled *The Psychology of the Psychic* by David Marks and Richard Kammann is a chapter called "The Roots of Coincidence," which puts forward a reasonably good proposition that might explain events as simple coincidence that some take to be paranormal, psychic, or spiritual. The argument begins with an illustration of a true story that happened to one of the authors. I quote the story so that there isn't any distortion:

> I usually forget my dreams, but seven years ago I had a particularly vivid and disturbing nightmare that turned out to be prophetic. In this dream, I kept running into the bathroom where my seven-year-old daughter was playing in the bathtub. The water level was not very high, but as dreams go, she had somehow shrunk to doll-size and was constantly slipping under the water, so I had to keep sitting her back up to keep her from drowning. I mentioned this bad dream to my wife the next day.
>
> After I had forgotten the dream, we were invited to a garden party at the home of friends who had a swimming pool. The party took place about two weeks later. After most of us had taken a dip in the pool, the adults gathered on the lawn for party talk and drinks. Suddenly out of the corner of my eye I saw my daughter thrashing under water in the deep end of the pool—she did not know how to swim. I broke through the crowd, jumped in beside her, and heaved her up into the arms of a friend at poolside. After a few gasps and

sputters, she got her breath back and was perfectly okay. She had been bobbing up and down alone in the shallow end of the pool and had drifted well beyond the ramp into the deep end.

After I was calm again I remembered the dream of saving her in the bathtub. Coincidence seemed impossible. Why should I, who rarely remember dreams, who never had a dream like that one, and who rarely went swimming with my daughter, find myself dreaming about her nearly drowning just two weeks before she nearly did? The idea of the pool party could not have caused the dream, because I remembered that the invitation came after it. The idea that the dream caused the pool incident seems absurd—if anything the dream should have made me more careful to prevent any accident. Nor could my memory of the dream have been revised to fit the facts, since I had already told it to my wife. After much discussion I could only guess that it was precognition, but whatever it was, I never forgot it.[1]

The authors then proceed to show that this is really just an "oddmatch"—that is, the dream as item A is related to the pool event as item B, and thus the two can be said to be related and "unexplained coincidence."[2] The authors continue by setting up probability theory and discussing the different types of coincidence as probability matches. The conclusion is simple: the swimming pool event was only a so-called oddmatch. The human error that might lead some to think of an otherworldly interface is simply the fact that "there are biases in human perception and reasoning that hide the role of probability from our view."

Related Events

Many chance happenings are indeed often interpreted as having a causal relationship. A child sees the stem of an apple snipped by scissors, and when the apple immediately plummets, the child concludes that the scissors caused the fall, although in fact it was gravity. It's very easy to jump to false conclusions. I remember a time when I awoke in the middle of the night after several tiny, somehow miniaturized people had just visited me and drilled in the left side of my chest. I intuitively knew they'd healed me in some way. I suspected it had to do with my left lung and the fact that I smoked three packs of cigarettes a day at the time. Whatever they'd done, I was confident it was beneficial.

Three days later, a woman visited one of my bookstores and asked to speak to me. I didn't know her, but had a staff member escort her upstairs to my office. She was dressed simply, and her behavior was calm and meek. Still, there was a great confidence about her and a special air that suggested she was quite at peace with herself and the world.

She told me of a project she was involved in and asked me to trust what she was about to tell me until I could see it for myself. She told me that she belonged to a group that sought to help others through a special method whereby they were reduced in size—miniaturized—and then sent to heal others. The leader of her group had taught this secret method to them, and they worked as much as possible in anonymity. She invited me to come see their group in the Utah desert and provided a map so that I could find their facility. I agreed to try to visit soon, and she left.

I shook my head when she was gone. Was this just a coincidence, or was it something else? I mean, how fantastic is it to expect that individuals under the guidance of some unnamed master are shrunk and sent to visit and heal others? The funny movie *Honey, I Shrunk the Kids* is almost more credible, isn't it?

As it turned out, I lost the map and was never able to verify what this woman told me. To this day, I wonder, *What are the odds of my dream and the woman's visit being just a coincidence?* I'd never read or thought of such a thing, and to the best of my knowledge, I've never known anyone familiar with this practice nor have I heard of it since. It's not exactly the same thing as bathtubs and swimming pools, or at least nowhere near as common. What does that mean?

No Such Thing as Paranormal

Edgar Mitchell, the Apollo 14 astronaut, once said "There are no natural or supernatural phenomena, only very large gaps in our knowledge of what is natural. We should strive to fill those gaps of ignorance." It's possible, as Marks and Kammann suggest in *The Psychology of the Psychic,* that—somewhere behind the scenes of both what we consider our knowledge and our methods of knowing—unidentified natural laws exist that could explain everything without calling upon some metaphysical realm per se. In a many-worlds way, I guess everything is technically possible, including that idea that Harry Potter really does live and J. K. Rowling just tapped into the story. That would be something like the Sci Fi channel's *Stargate* story in which Barber Joe taps into General Jack O'Neill's stories without knowing that O'Neill is real, and that what made this possible was a special interdimensional device.

I don't know that this is really credible, but obviously some opt for it while choosing to disregard the possibility that there's a metaphysical explanation that invokes some spiritual reality. Personally, I look for cues in the information that comes to me, and I suspect that there's a connected pattern somewhere. This approach suggests a low likelihood for pure coincidence.

For example, one day when I was with a young woman who worked for me, she pointed to an airplane high in the sky. I squinted and could barely make out what might be an aircraft. She asked if I could see the skydivers about to jump. I answered, "Sure," or something along those lines, in a tone that said, "Like anyone could actually see that from here." She was serious, however. She could see the jumpers, and soon I saw parachutes opening. This woman truly had the proverbial eagle eyes.

A few weeks later, I was running surveillance on a case, and she was the spotter while I drove. We were looking for a child who'd been abducted from a grocery store in the area. As I turned onto a street with one of the addresses we were checking, this woman suddenly shouted, "There she is!" I looked at the house in question (which was a few houses up from the bottom of the street) but saw nothing. I stopped the car and asked for an explanation. My employee told me that as we turned the corner, a little girl was looking out the front window from behind the drapes, and she quickly ducked back as the car entered the street. If I hadn't known of this woman's vision from the incident with the skydivers I wouldn't have acted, but I trusted her, and sure enough we recovered the child.

More Visions

I was in New York City attending the American Booksellers' convention in the early '90s. In the middle of the night before I was to return to my office in Las Vegas, I awoke for no reason. I tried to go back to sleep, but to no avail, so I finally got up and started my day. I caught my plane on time and landed just as planned. I proceeded without hesitation to the luggage area and then to ground transportation. That's when it hit me: *Where was my business partner and closest friend, Roy Bey?* He was always waiting at the gate (in those days you could still do this). He was my transportation. My stomach turned suddenly, and I knew he'd passed over.

A cab ride home verified this knowledge. In the recliner in his bedroom was my friend. He'd passed over while taking a nap late the day before. To this day, I'm certain that somewhere in the back of my mind, perhaps deep in my subconscious, was the knowledge of Roy's earthly departure. I didn't look for him at the gate, and I didn't page him. I didn't even think about anything until it was time to head out of the airport. Roy always picked me up. We'd done this kind of thing many, many times before. It was routine. I had to have known. Is that coincidence?

Roy's Birth

When my wife, Ravinder, and I decided to have children, I knew that the first would be a boy. I proposed naming him in memory of my

96

friend Roy Bey (who appears in more stories from the past throughout the rest of this book), and Ravinder agreed. She chose to have natural-birth training and to deliver at our home in Big Bear, California. This should have made me very nervous because her midwife lived down the hill in Redlands and the due date was in November. Big Bear could have heavy snowstorms that time of the year, which made travel in the area difficult, if not impossible.

On November 20 around midnight, Ravinder's water broke. We called the midwife, who came right to our home, as did one of Ravinder's friends. The next morning, they took my wife for a walk. All day the midwife, her assistant, and my wife's female friend encouraged her, walked with her, talked to her, and so on until finally everyone gave up around nine o'clock on the evening of the 21st. Somehow I'd known that the child was a boy and that he'd be born on November 22. I had told Ravinder and the midwife this, but no one listened.

On November 21 just before midnight, I was urged to get Ravinder out of bed. She trusted me, so she got up, and together we began her efforts to increase the labor. The midwife and her helpers weren't pleased with my intervention, but soon the midwife's supervisor came to my rescue. She'd driven up the hill because she was concerned about my wife's lack of progress. Ravinder asked me how much longer as she pressed against me with another contraction. I told her 10 to 15 minutes and had her stand and hold on to me. The supervisor checked and confirmed with Ravinder that 15 minutes seemed about right.

The long and the short of it is this: Ravinder dilated from three centimeters to ten and gave birth to our son, Roy Kenneth, 14 minutes after I gave her my estimate. His umbilical cord was dry when I cut it just a moment or two later. Obviously, Ravinder couldn't have carried him any longer and still given birth to a healthy child. Roy was born just as I'd been told—on November 22, at 12:34 AM. Is this a coincidence?

Road Trip

When our son Roy was about 18 months old, we decided to move from California to Washington. We were relocating our home and business, so we hired movers, but we still were left having to drive separately. I planned to drive the truck with its camper, loaded with our large puppy and cat, and pull our boat. Ravinder would drive the car, taking with her Roy and some of our plants. I was very nervous about the journey because it was some distance and Ravinder was still getting accustomed to driving in America. (She often approached the car from the wrong side, intending to drive on the left as they do in the United Kingdom, where we met.) I purchased a good set of walkie-talkies and did some predrive coaching. I continued to be concerned, but I was told by the voice within that everything would be fine—Ravinder and Roy would be taken care of. I accepted the reassurance and gave thanks.

We started our drive early in the morning, and as we descended the mountain toward Redlands, I swerved to miss a rock in the road and immediately warned Ravinder of it. I couldn't see whether she cleared it or not, so I asked her. She said that she'd hit it, but everything was okay.

We drove all day and that evening checked into a motel along the highway. The next morning, I went outside to load some of the luggage we'd taken into the motel the night before. As I walked to the trunk of my wife's car, I couldn't help but see the damage to the right rear tire. It was not only flat but shredded, with most of it off the rim; and the rim itself was badly bent. How was that possible? Well, it simply isn't!

Ravinder drove 55 to 70 miles an hour, following me all the way down the canyon, through Los Angeles, and up the coast for at least eight hours. Even if the original rock wasn't the culprit, it was easy to see from the tire that it had blown during the drive. There's no way anyone could have driven that car through a blowout and gone on, seriously bending the rim beyond repair, without being aware that something was wrong.

What would you say happened? What does that mean? Again, is this just a coincidence?

Communications

One evening while deeply asleep, I heard a voice call out to me. I opened my eyes but saw no one there. I'd received the impression of the word *fire,* so I got out of bed and went downstairs. There was the kitchen towel I'd left on the edge of the electric range. A burner was on, and the fabric ignited just as I stepped into the room. I grabbed the towel and threw it into the sink, where running water quickly turned the flames into smelly smoke. I turned the burner off, stood there a moment, and said "Thank you" as I glanced up at the ceiling as though looking through it and far beyond. Then I went back to bed. Coincidence? If not, then what was it?

One night I was coming back from a speaking engagement in Rock Springs, Wyoming, and knew that my business partner Roy Bey would be worried about my late return. I'd been unable to reach him at my condo, where he was staying while visiting from Chicago. I tried to send him a message like the one my father had sent to my mother all those years ago: just a simple "Don't worry." We were best friends as well as colleagues, and he thought of himself as my older brother and even as a father figure, so it wasn't unusual for him to worry. I finally stopped trying to send him a message when I came upon a herd of antelope slowly crossing the road. The suddenness of their appearance was like a banging on my dreary state of consciousness at 3 A.M. as I drove a so-called shortcut home. I thought that I needed to pay more attention to the road and less to sending some mental message.

When I did get home around 5 A.M., Roy was up having coffee. We chatted, and then he told me that he'd been a little worried until about three o'clock when the washing machine began banging in the laundry room. He got up, could see no reason why it would suddenly start running, let alone begin banging as though the spin cycle needed balancing; but he knew it was a message from me, telling him I was okay. Another coincidence?

More Guidance

At a time when I was intending to relocate my business, I traveled to Texas and Montana, looking at block-grant opportunities and other offers designed to entice us to move. I was unable to make a decision. Then one night while I was sound asleep, my bed shook. I sat up, and there at the end of the bed stood a tall, stern male figure who said to me: "The only place for you to be is Las Vegas, Nevada."

The next morning I went to my office and announced that we were heading to Las Vegas. My partner was overjoyed, for that was where he'd wanted to go all along, but a key member of my staff immediately balked at the idea. To make a long story short, this person tried to stop the move. In time we discovered why, and unearthed information we never would have found otherwise. The fact is, there were shortages and accounting irregularities that, had they not been brought to light, would have put us out of business. We could have moved almost anywhere, and it wouldn't have been a problem for this person, but Las Vegas was an issue because of the individual's history. In other words, Las Vegas was the only place I could move and discover the threat to the company in time to save it. Again—was this just another coincidence?

I could go on with stories from my own life, and I'll share more throughout the rest of the book, but I suppose you could call all of this coincidence anyway, couldn't you? *Do* you? How many such events have you experienced? Most people have had quite a few, but for some reason they simply forget about them until something prompts the memory to reemerge. What does that mean?

◈◈◈ ◈◈◈

chapter 14

ENLIGHTENMENT

"I sometimes think that God, in creating man,
somewhat overestimated his ability."
— **Oscar Wilde**

There's an old saying: "Enlightenment comes in the dark." Many tend to think that enlightenment is a special state of consciousness that, once achieved, releases some or all the restrictions of mortality. For me, that simply isn't so. In my mind, it's a waking-up process that comes as a result of spiritually evolving, a little bit at a time.

What do you think enlightenment is? Would you know it if you met it? A story about the Buddha implies that it's an easily seen state of being. The story goes like this:

A man comes upon the Buddha while traveling one day. He falls to his knees and says, "You must be a god."

The Buddha, facing him, replies, "No, I'm not a god."

The traveler then insists that the Buddha must be a demigod.

Again the Buddha says no.

Finally, the traveler falls back in despair and asks, "Then what are you?"

The Buddha answers, "Awake."

Is being awake enlightenment? Is it visible? If you met an enlightened person, would you recognize their state of being?

Hermann Hesse's delightful book *Siddhartha* tells the story of how the title character meets the Buddha. Siddhartha has studied long and learned the ways of the Jain shramanas (contemplative hermits, or anchorites). His asceticism has given him a special insight to the ways of humankind. He has gained power over his body and is able to control his heartbeat, his body temperature, and more. Siddhartha does immediately recognize something unusual about the Buddha—a special sort of consciousness that sets him apart. It's an at-peace sense of consciousness or personal air. Siddhartha has sought a teacher who *is* what he teaches and has finally found such an individual—yet Siddhartha immediately recognizes that listening to or being with the Buddha is not *being* the Buddha. Sadly, Siddhartha withdraws.

His journey and many years of study with the masters led him to what he thought he wanted, only for him to realize that he didn't wish to have a teacher who was enlightened—rather, he wanted to be enlightened himself. All the words of Buddha couldn't accomplish this; he had to transform himself. In that moment of realization, Siddhartha is reenergized, for he understands that although he has sought enlightenment everywhere, he hasn't looked inward. He has run away from himself in pursuit of something that could only really be found within. With this new realization, he begins seeking knowledge of himself and the world he lives in.

Dark Night of the Soul

The story of Siddhartha is a wonderful and still relevant story, so I won't spoil it by telling you more. I've shared this much to introduce my own experience with enlightenment. Unlike Siddhartha, I wasn't born a Brahman and my father wasn't rich. Like Siddhartha, I did leave home. I went from being a devout young follower to being an agnostic, potentially atheistic antagonist of religiosity; and I finally moved toward the spiritual evolution I'm experiencing today. I began to study comparative religion and secret orders. I looked into various mystical systems and sampled a variety of practices. I even studied to become a minister. Let me digress, however, if you will.

There came a point in my life that I sought more meaning. The question *Is this all there is?* haunted me. Events led me to examine myself more fully, and in the process I witnessed just how petty and selfish I was. For me, this was a dark night of the soul. Indeed, it was partially a real night when I drove across four states. I began in Utah, drove to Nevada, into Arizona, and then down to California, all in one day and night. I took the trip in order to think—to get some things straight in my mind. What I received was more than I bargained for and too personal to disclose fully in this context. Suffice it to say, I saw my innermost selfish, insecure, petty, controlling, and manipulative self in action as I reviewed deed after deed. By daybreak, I was absolutely disgusted with myself. I pledged to do better and begged for the opportunity to do just that.

The Fruit of the Tree

I must tell you that before my "dark night" I had an earlier experience that I thought validated my path at the time. So let me backtrack and tell you a story about why I thought I had things in order.

When I finished my bachelor-level studies with the University of Metaphysics, I was sent ordination papers. I looked over the documents and set them down. I knew I wasn't a minister. I was hotheaded, sometimes ill-tempered, less than courteous to many, and otherwise anything but what a minister is supposed to be. As a boy I'd stolen, and as a man I'd often lied. I sometimes enjoyed hurting people, physically or emotionally, just to hurt them. The idea that somehow I

103

was ready to become a minister simply didn't sit well with me. At the same time, I longed to continue my studies, for they'd brought me much peace, but I couldn't go on unless I took the ordination vows.

Troubled, my mind full of stuff I really didn't want, I lay down on the sofa for a nap and dreamed. When I awoke, I wrote down the dream. It was a turning point for me, yet it wasn't just *my* dream, for it has been shared by many. Here's what I experienced:

It all began with a man looking within himself. He said, "I desire to serve God, but my life has been full of error. The example I have set is not that of a cleric. People will only scoff and say, 'Know ye them by the fruits of their tree.' Who am I, then, to speak for or of God?"

With these words circling within his head, the troubled man lay down to rest. He spoke to God: "Your will, not mine, be done."

As he drifted into sleep, pictures began appearing that told this story:

Once there stood a tree—a tree of life, full of fruit. The limbs bent toward the earth under the weight of lush red cherries. They danced jubilantly in the breeze that bathed their tender skins and turned their fullness and vivid color to face the Father, the sun of the heavens.

With the dew and the rain, they polished their beauty and drank of the earth, storing within them the energy and vitality of life taken from the soil through the tree's roots. They were aglow with the spirit of the sun radiating through the leaves of their parent tree.

But alas, not all of the children of the tree would mature into lush red fruit. Out of an urge to experience and learn on his own, one turned away from the Father and ignored the parental warnings. Charlie, as the other cherries knew him, kept his life juices warm, daring the cold, the frost, and the elements. He began to fill with color and mature early.

Pivoting on his base, he turned away from the sun and took shelter in the shade of the leaves. Daring to fornicate with the world, Charlie refused to release the natural pesticides within himself and took up affairs with the parasites.

Soon his delicate skin was broken, and his fruit exposed. The fragrance attracted the birds; and they, too, feasted on him. Charlie lived off the flesh and the world. Passion, experience, and knowledge were his prizes.

Then one day the gardener came. Gently he took from the parent tree the pure and ripened children, leaving only Charlie behind. Hanging alone, Charlie looked about him. The fall nights were cold and lonely. His friends the birds were on the wing, abandoning him. His flesh had spoiled, and even the insects avoided him now. His soul hung onto his tattered body. The elements he'd once faced with a thrill now threatened to snap him from the stem of life. Charlie was sad and lonely. He'd learned these things: knowledge isn't necessarily wisdom; experience isn't always a kind teacher; and passion can be a poison that betrays whatever value there is to be had in experience and knowledge.

Charlie looked up at the beautiful blue sky and the buoyant white clouds adrift, seemingly without anything to do or a care in the world, lazily sailing across the vast heavens. *They and the lilies of the field . . . ,* Charlie said to himself.

"Dear God," he spoke aloud, "I have sinned. I've wasted the beauty of your flower and turned my back on simple truth. In my pursuit of wisdom, I lost sight of Your Great Form and indulged in physical illusions. I am lost. I alone am to blame. I give my essence over to thee, Creator of all that is good within me and all that could ever be love within me. For You are eternal love, and what's best for me is also your way. That I should only discover this now is my most significant regret.

"I've watched the caterpillar spin his cocoon and perch on the leaves above me as a butterfly," Charlie continued, "but I fear that this recognition has come so late in my life that I'll be unable to share this beauty, this truth, with others."

Suddenly, a squirrel jerked Charlie from the limb and scampered down the tree and across the meadow. The squirrel paused, examined the battered fruit, and then—as though rejecting him—dropped him in the grass.

Charlie rested there for a day or two, and then the snow came. Covered by the white blanket, he slept.

The seasons passed as though in the twinkling of an eye. Charlie took root and grew strong. From his branches came blossoms, followed by fruit more beautiful than he could ever remember beholding.

Charlie praised God and gave thanks.

The lowly man in my dream raised his head from slumber. His prayer had been answered. The Lord doesn't forsake humankind; humans forsake the Lord. He thought, *Thy will, not mine, be done; for after all, in their eternal boundless beauty, they are one and the same.* And then I woke up.

I won't even ask this time what it all means—I'll let you do whatever asking there is to be done. I'll let you decide what enlightenment is, as well. Perhaps, like me, you'll come to the conclusion that it's a dynamic process that evolves the entire being—mind, body, and spirit.

chapter 15

THE REAL ME

*"When people are free to do as they please,
they usually imitate each other."*
— Eric Hoffer

What's in a name? We tend to think we know something if we can name it. "Who's that over there?" someone asks. "Oh, that's Martha," comes the answer. Does that really tell us who Martha is? A child asks how lightbulbs work, and we answer by informing him that electricity lights the bulb when we flick the switch. Does that really say anything meaningful?

Who am I? Who is the "I" the question is about? "I" is certainly not my name. For example, I'm Eldon Taylor. Does that really say who I am? Let's try again: I am Dr. Eldon Taylor. There, now I've modified it some. Do you know any more about me? The answer is not really, even though it might seem so. All that's been added is the implication that I have had some schooling—but in what? Despite this, we tend to make judgments about people based on their names and titles. So Barack Obama's middle name, *Hussein,* became a problem during his presidential campaign because it brought to mind Saddam Hussein.

My friend Joseph Error shared a true story that makes this point eloquently. He's a group leader at Oak Ridge National Laboratory, an applied research and development facility. Here's his story:

> A couple of years ago, I went to Switzerland to attend a conference on precision measuring equipment. One of the attendees from Europe was a man with the last name "Loser." He was a brilliant physicist/engineer who developed an instrument in the late '80s that is still the standard in the world for long-distance measuring. The device, referred to as a ME000 Mekometer, can accurately record linear measurement to better than .2 millimeters per kilometer. Although the instrument itself is now a bit long in the tooth and somewhat cumbersome to operate, for pure measuring accuracy it has never been surpassed.
>
> At any rate, at the banquet, one of the keynote speakers mentioned that sitting at table five were two interesting individuals: one built the Mekometer, and the second was in charge of the alignment of the world's most expensive scientific project. Amazingly, their last names were "Loser" and "Error." The observation brought a lot of good-natured cheers from the crowd. I guess there's a moral in there somewhere.

Obviously there's more to a person, an animal, a thing, or anything that we can and do name than the name itself implies. Indeed, as has been pointed out by many people, once you name something, you begin to subtract from it, for what you say it *is* also implies what it can*not* be.

Just Space

What if you discovered that you were the space in your body, not the matter? Indeed, imagine that everyone you know—everyone everywhere, in fact—is space, not matter. Subtract the matter, and what's left is space touching space. A sort of nothingness—and eventually homogenous space—each still an individual but at the same time all a part of one. Like a drop of water in the ocean, each drop unique yet a part of the whole in an indistinguishable way. Space, not water, merging with other space . . .

The atom consists of very little matter. In fact, it's 99 percent free space. The nucleus of an atom has been compared to a marble in an area the size of a large stadium with the closest electron being as far away as the most distant seats. Physicists insist that wherever there's mass, there is energy; thus the famous equation $E = mc^2$. That is, mass and energy are interchangeable. What if, when you leave your body—however you might do that, including at death—what's left is space defined or somehow framed as energy. Just space, but energized in some way. Conscious space, perhaps, but emptiness all the same, able to merge with all other voids. What would you call this space? If you named it, would it make anything clearer or would it just complicate matters?

Think of the soul, the spirit, the oversoul, and all the other names that are designed to inform us of who we really are at a quintessential level. Do they add or subtract from our understanding? You know it's been said that God plagued man with the ability to think. Is it the thinking or the naming that torments us? How can we really know ourselves?

The Process of Elimination

Sometimes the best way to discover what something is comes from eliminating what it isn't. This can be an arduous task. Think, for example, of how you might explain electricity to a child if you approached it this way. Still, this is an important avenue by which we can approach our real selves.

We are not our names. We should also assume for the moment that we are not just physical creatures that have evolved as a result of some random chaotic event. Does that mean, then, that we're eternal? Our psychology is such that the subconscious tells the conscious mind what to think, makes most of our decisions, marshals the evidence when we sort matters out, and so forth. The subconscious is also the home of our defense mechanisms, and they must be hidden from the conscious mind if they're to work. Our minds have been programmed or propagandized from birth by parents, peers, social conventions, media, salespeople, politicians, and more.

Yet the word *enculturation* means much more today than it did in the 20th century, for it must include the digital world. For digital natives (those who've never experienced a time when mobile phones, iPods and other mp3 players, video games, computers, and so forth didn't exist), just existing in the world means constant contact with anyone, anywhere and also limited attention—simply because there are so many things to give partial attention to. For nonnatives, the digital pace has forced changes in how we communicate and know our world.

The information age is responsible for the input into many minds, which is often accepted in a nondiscriminatory way. Take, for example, television. The average person will enter an alpha brain-wave state after less than five minutes in front of the television. This is akin to hypnosis in that the mind is hyper-suggestible. In addition, the information is absorbed without thought. Huge amounts of data are programmed into it and without conscious attention to what's being absorbed.

Who Am I?

All of this tells me that knowing myself—the real me—isn't a simple or easy task. It seems that I can't take my own interpretations at face value because my subconscious may well have a motive to fool me. Additionally, I know that the way I dress, the way I stand, the clothes I wear, the hairstyle I choose, the language I speak and think in, the values and beliefs I hold, and so much more have all been given to me by the world I live in. So answering *Who am I?* may well require subtracting *Who I am not* at the outset of any search for my real self.

When we strip away the various name tags used to define us, everything changes. As René Descartes once did, when we try to view ourselves as purely thinking agents with no body or physical component, it's easy to succumb to the notion of mind-body dualism.[1] That is, the

110

mental stuff is independent of the physical stuff, yet common sense may make us wonder *How do we think without the brain?*

I suggest that when stripping everything away, think of yourself as space. This is not to say that you're space alone; rather, it's a powerful metaphor that can open up your discovery of who you really are. Considering yourself as space, imagine your *self* reflecting on you, on life, on the meaning of it all. Expand your *self,* merging your space into more and more space, growing ever larger until you've expanded to contain the entire universe. From this perspective you become all things—no thing and every thing.

I think of this as the experience of approaching zero divided by zero. (Take any number and divide it by smaller and smaller fractions, and you'll find that the answer becomes larger and larger. In other words, the closer you get to zero, the larger your answer becomes.) This is a proposition I came to and wrote about long before encountering the work of some of the great mathematicians and metaphysicians. It's such a natural idea that I'm sure many have arrived at it intuitively. The bottom line of the exercise is this: Who are you now? It has been said that in the beginning there was one, and the one divided itself and created all.

Fixers and Fixes

There are many fixers in the world, and even more fixes. If any one of us needs to be fixed, we can find a variety of ways to do that. But for many of those who gorge themselves on all the solutions, the only thing accomplished is eliminating one more option so that they can go on to the next fix.

When exit polls are conducted after motivational events, we find that the majority of respondents report that this is the thing for them. This experience awakened them and will change their lives. They've found the magic potion, and it all came about in this wonderful day or two. When we look at follow-up data from 30 and 60 days later, however, we find that very, very few attendees have actually used what they learned. The reported reasons vary from simple procrastination to lengthy explanations of how, upon reflection, the system just wasn't right for their personalities. You may have experienced something similar.

The root cause for these disappointing results is simple: The subconscious mind differed from what you consciously thought. Perhaps defense mechanisms stopped you or false beliefs led to self-sabotaging action or inaction, or perhaps it was a matter of self-image and risk. In other words, the simple conscious choice, if we can call it that, is often not enough to make you change. Again I ask, *How then can you know yourself?*

What does this mean? Do you truly know yourself? Does it matter? What would it mean if you did?

chapter 16

AIRY FAIRIES, WHINY WIMPS, AND SCANDALOUS SHAMANS

"To you everything that's happening in the world appears phony,
to be something other than what it really is, right?"
— attributed to **J. D. Salinger**

When I'd evolved enough in my own life to find room for spiritual matters and even for parapsychological ones, there were still fringe things I could only laugh at. When Shirley MacLaine, an actress I really thought was hot, wrote *Out on a Limb,* the only thing I could say was that she not only went out on a limb but she cut the thing off the tree while she was out there. I thought it was an absolutely airy-fairy story. UFOs visiting Earth and bringing enlightenment was just too much for me at the time.

Sometime later, I met an Apache shaman named Taco while doing a radio show in Salt Lake City. We became friends and often spent time together off the air. From him, I learned that bogus shamans are as common as the Indian gurus looking to gain from tourists— there's practically one on every corner. *Scandalous,* I thought, *to prey on others' spiritual vulnerabilities.*

Testing the Psychic

Before meeting Taco, I'd played around with crystal wands to test some of the ideas that my physicist friend David Maerze had suggested. I knew that the semiprecious stone lapis lazuli was used in the cockpits of jet aircraft because of its uncanny ability to help pilots eliminate dizziness, so testing other rocks and crystals made sense. David had worked for the government, and he was making special tools from crystal. So I thought, *If he'd risk his reputation, what do I have to lose?*

I built several crystal wands using various designs, including hollow copper rods into which I inserted batteries or cattle magnets or both, and used them to carry out various experiments. One day I was at a psychic fair, where a pretty woman was doing psychic readings. I approached her for a session, and we ended up chatting for some time. She told me that the only thing she could suggest for me was to stop eating green beans so that I'd become stronger on inner levels. (I admit that to this day I tend to avoid the vegetable, even though I'm consciously convinced that this was just so much nonsense.)

During our conversation, she promised to stop by my bookstore one day and look me up (at that time my business offices were in the back). One day she did stop in, and a staff member came back to tell me she was there. I went out to greet her, but she was with a man, which wasn't what I expected. She was checking out some of the wands I'd built and put in the display case. She asked what they were and how to use them. Instead of giving her the lengthy and truthful explanation, I simply said, "They magnify your conscious energy, what you *will*, into creation. Let me show you."

I went back to my office and removed a wand full of cattle magnets from my desk drawer. I also took a compass from my desk and then returned to the front of the store, where I placed the compass on the glass case. Then, squinting my eyes as though deep in concentration, I turned the wand toward the compass and said, "Move." It rotated wildly, of course.

I told her: "Choose a wand out of the case and try it. Just concentrate your mental energy totally into the wand and you'll see just how much you can magnify that energy. Once you have the wand that's right for you, don't let others handle it. You want your energy—and only yours—in it. You especially, because of your psychic gifts, will be able to do this without difficulty."

I then instructed a staff member to help her choose a wand, excused myself for a minute on the pretense of checking in on a meeting already in progress, and returned to my office with my magnetized wand.

If you haven't guessed already, none of the wands in the glass case had magnets or anything else in them. They were simply copper rods wrapped in leather, with a crystal—sometimes a double terminated one—fitted into one end. The other end of each piece had a simple copper cap on it, so that customers could put whatever they wanted into the hollow tube.

Well, the psychic tried and tried to use the wands, but to no avail. The compass just wouldn't move. She whined and whimpered and huffed and puffed, but nothing happened. She left frustrated and embarrassed, and I never saw her again.

Now, I don't tell that story because I'm proud of it—indeed, it's embarrassing to think that I was so insensitive and self-centered. I share it only because there's so much out there that fails the tests of honest skeptics. That's the problem with coming to grips with or understanding the real nature of mystical and parapsychological endeavors and abilities. These phenomena are often scoffed at, because many people claiming the special powers are not genuine.

Convincing the Doubting Thomas

As a doubting Thomas, so to speak, I still had to explain the many extraordinary phenomena that filled my own life. To compound this challenge, I had an experience while working with crystals that defied normal explanations.

I was meditating one day when the breastplate of Aaron came into my mind. The Bible tells its story and indicates that whoever wore it had special healing power and more. I was familiar with the tale, and it seemed clear to me that Aaron's breastplate was for a specific time and a specific person, but for some reason I also knew that I could have my own version. I opened my eyes following the meditation and jotted down some notes. Later that day, I found a book in my store that detailed various gemstones and their alleged powers or gifts. I began to design my own breastplate using my notes and this book.

Things didn't come together properly—or at least they didn't feel right—so I set the project aside and forgot about it for a couple of weeks. Then one afternoon, again while I was meditating, a representation of the breastplate appeared in my mind. Startled, I opened my eyes and drew what I'd seen to the best of my ability. Over the following few weeks, I searched out the stones that would lie in the circuit as I'd seen it, each positioned as though it were an on/off switch for a different function. As I worked with the drawing and the stones, I made it a practice to confirm my choices by meditating until I was certain I had it right. Then I got stuck.

One of the gems had to be padparadscha, a rare specimen found only in India. If that wasn't enough of a problem, it was illegal to remove the stone from its native country. However, I learned never to underestimate the power of friends.

It's sometimes risky to confide your fringe inquiries and findings with others, but when you do so, you may be surprised by what you find. As I opened up and began sharing, people I never expected to be open to this kind of thing stepped forward. I shared my problem and the project with a wonderful friend of mine who didn't have a lot to say but was supportive. Within a couple of weeks, she stopped by and brought me a padparadscha the perfect size and shape for the breastplate. She refused to tell me where or how she'd acquired the stone and wouldn't accept any payment. By that point, all I needed was a special artisan to make the design exactly as I'd seen it. I had the materials, but where would I find the artisan?

I've learned that when you need something, ask! I asked the Universe to bring me the craftsperson, and sure enough, it did. A young woman came into my store looking for a job. She was hired to work in the office, and then I learned she was a jeweler by hobby and that her mother was a shaman. This presented the perfect opportunity, so I asked her if she could do what I had in mind, and when she said yes, I handed the project to her.

My new employee took a couple of months to complete the work. She had some difficulty engraving the circuit pattern and indeed experienced an acid spill that led her mother to exclaim about the potential harm that could come from the breastplate. In fact, her mom insisted that the device was bad.

When it was completed, I took a morning off work to dedicate it. It was in the early summer, and I invited my son and daughter to join me. Holding the breastplate to the sky, conscious of all that I'd come to understand it was, I spoke its blessing aloud on my patio. Suddenly, the sky went dark, and hail stormed down, forcing us inside. The hail was exceptionally large and broke the glass on the outdoor light fixtures.

That evening, the local news reported a small but intense hailstorm centered over the area where I lived. The broadcasters commented about the improbability of such a storm and the unusual size of the hail. For some reason, I didn't feel that the storm was the bearer of bad tidings in any way, nor do I now. It was my understanding that the breastplate, as created for me, worked with the elements, perhaps even had some control over them, as I'd indicated in the dedication language.

Clearing the Snow

A few months later, my partner Roy Bey and I were scheduled to be in Logan, Utah, for a presentation when a significant snowstorm beset the area. Logan is near the Wyoming border, and the region is known for record snow and the accompanying bad roads. Nevertheless, we left Salt Lake City and soon found ourselves dealing with a heavy winter storm. I put my hand on the breastplate, which at that time I wore continually, and thought of clear roads—of snow falling around us but not on us. "Clear the way," were my half-muttered words.

Roy asked what I'd said, and I told him what I was trying to do. He was a scientist, an engineer by profession and education, and I'm sure he often had his doubts about me and some of my ways, but he didn't voice them on this occasion.

We drove to Logan through the storm on wet roads with snow falling in front of, behind, and on both sides of us all the way there. The presentation took about three hours, after which we returned to Salt Lake City. Snow lay all around us, but the roads before us were only slightly wet. The next morning, the reported accumulation of several inches on the roads made us shake our heads. When we'd stepped outside the night before, the ground was covered with several inches of snow, yet we had clear roads all the way home. How is that possible?

Mind Is Not a Local Event

Is it possible that each of us possesses special knowledge, and that from time to time we truly do experience epiphanies of a metaphysical sort? Or are we just dealing with coincidence, Pygmalion factors, self-fulfilling prophecies, and the like? Is it a matter of psychic hoaxes, airy-fairy nonsense, whiny wimps with pleadings and warnings designed to frighten us into believing certain things, and scandalous shamans out to take our money and belongings?

Today, physicists teach us that the universe is nonlocal. In my book *Choices and Illusions,* I spent time on the notion that *mind is not a local event,* which has been repeatedly demonstrated by science. For example, taking cells from the body and dividing them into two groups, moving one set several miles from the other, and then shocking one of the groups with low-voltage electricity will result in both groups reacting simultaneously as though they were still together.[1] With respect to matter, if you separate two paired particles and give one of them a downward spin, the other will instantly spin upward, and this relationship will remain regardless of the distance that separates the two.[2]

If matter itself is only energy vibrating at different rates and if, as physicists insist, nothing is ever lost, then the nonlocal nature and interrelated necessity of all things becomes suddenly easier to understand. For as the strings of the universe vibrate, the entire universe resonates; and as with two pianos in the same room, if you strike a note on one, the second instrument will sound the note in resonance. Does that suggest that minds could communicate across distance or that other energies, including elemental, could vibrate through some similar mechanism?

Time is a part of the space continuum. That is to say, time and space are one unit, inseparable, according to modern physics. Is time subject to "mind stuff"?

Time Travel

One Saturday in 1988, I had a noon meeting in St. George, Utah. The people were seriously interested in opening a Mind Mint bookstore (a franchise owned by Roy and myself) in their town, and the appointment had been made more than a week earlier. Still, I was called to my office in Salt Lake City early that beautiful day for an urgent meeting that lasted until midmorning. I looked at my watch as I drove onto the freeway. It was just a minute or two before 10 A.M. I had to be in St. George in two hours, and it was a five-hour drive. Not possible.

From the moment I entered the freeway to the time I got to my destination, I imagined seeing myself arrive and looking at a clock that said exactly 12 noon. I held this image in my mind almost to the exclusion of all else.

I was in a new Chrysler, and I knew the route very well. I remember going by an overpass somewhere around Beaver, Utah, and being aware of my speed, but I kept right on driving, focused on arriving at noon. As I walked into what was to become our St. George store, there on the wall was a large clock that said 12. This was so extraordinary that I had to point out to those in St. George and those I'd met with in Salt Lake City that somehow the 300 miles that separated my office from the prospective bookstore had melted away in two hours. To this day, I can't explain how that happened—but I guarantee you that it did! How is that possible? And what does it mean?

The Enquiry

Also in 1988, I began holding what I called Enquiry Meetings after hours in one of our bookstores. All who attended could bring any question they wanted, and together we attempted to derive some meaningful answers. The group quickly had a preponderance of professional people, many of whom held graduate degrees. One evening, a general-systems theorist introduced us all to what he called the Asisus—as-is-us—an elaborate geometric grid that arguably underlies all creation. We played with many possibilities and finally decided to use it as a sort of psionic device (a mental amplifier). We then decided to meet on a Saturday morning and run a short experiment.

On the specified day, my friend Jim, who has a Ph.D. in chemistry, and I became the subjects; and according to those present, we disappeared. Although it was for just a few brief seconds, the witnesses said we really did disappear, despite the fact that Jim and I noticed no change in our physical experience. Both of us were meditating, eyes closed, on the Asisus geometric grid. We pictured ourselves walking from the outside of the grid inward.

Later that week, Jim phoned me from the university. He'd been meditating when the phone rang. He reached for it on the desk, but when his hand didn't find the phone, he looked down and saw that his hand was actually through the top of the desk and into the top drawer. This startled him, and he immediately withdrew his hand. He then phoned to tell me what had happened.

How is this possible?

A Metaphysical Epiphany

When we look back on our lives, is what we see an outline or blueprint of who we are? As we've discussed, we aren't our names, credentials, or jobs, yet we're all of those things in some way. Our unique purpose or meaning isn't for someone else to give us. It's for us to learn and know. Just as with fancy motivational seminars, all the tools anyone else can provide are only tools. I can't do anyone's breathing except my own, nor can you. Knowing ourselves is all there is to know—or is it?

Psychotherapist Ann Jauregui shows us in her book *Epiphanies* that most people, if not all, hold somewhere in their memory a metaphysical epiphany, a moment when through some means a special insight that suspended time and space was experienced.[3] She also suggests that if we tended such experiences as we might tend a garden, rather than forgetting them and failing to share them, they could make a dramatic difference in our lives. Do you remember any such experience in your life? Did you give it special attention?

I haven't tended all of mine, and quite frankly, I sometimes think the Universe has every reason to just give up on me. Still, with great patience it continues to be there.

I believe that everyone has experiences that aren't easily explained, but for whatever reason, we tend to shove them to the back of our minds. However, it's these very events that are the doorway to the higher meaning of life. Whatever they signify, the meaning is important for all of us.

❖❖❖ ❖❖❖

chapter 17

VIOLENCE

"The world is a dangerous place to live, not because of the people who are evil, but because of the people who don't do anything about it."
— **Albert Einstein**

The idea that minds create seems to be something that I've always known intuitively, so when the notion of like attracting like was first introduced to me, it seemed natural and true. Extending this to the notion that our minds create the world we live in through projection was both metaphysically easy and intellectually possible, given our ethnocentric enculturation and our perceptual processes. (We see our implicit assumptions about the world rather than see the real world for what it is. These assumptions are the result of our enculturation and therefore our expectations.) As such, adding a little unconditional love to this recipe should yield a peaceful answer to the problems of the world.

That is, as Deepak Chopra told Shawn Hannity on the Fox News Network in November 2008, there would be no violence in the world if people committed their thoughts to peace. When questioned further by Hannity regarding evil in the world and what he'd do if his daughter or wife were being attacked or raped, Chopra replied that it wouldn't happen to him because he creates a serene environment that surrounds him and defuses the necessity or desire for violence. Chopra went on to describe a time when he talked four teenagers out of attacking him.

These opposing viewpoints—Hannity with his belief in evil versus Chopra with his belief in unconditional surrender in the way of Gandhi—have been a thorny problem for me most of my life. Is there evil in the world, or is what we see as evil a part of our projection?

Gandhi and the Taliban

One of my heroes is Gandhi, yet I cannot see his tactics working with al-Qaeda or the Taliban. Why is that?

Think about it for a minute: The English are a proud people, and Gandhi's tactics embarrassed them into relinquishing control in India. For England, of all nations, to respond to unarmed protestors by brutally beating them one after another until hundreds lay on the ground, was just more than the conscience of that nation could bear. How does that compare to a group of thugs who'd publicly stone a woman or decapitate an unarmed member of the press?

A rabbi and his wife were visiting a Jewish center in India just hours before Americans celebrated Thanksgiving. Terrorists stormed through the doors of the center and gunned them down, along with a 13-year-old girl visiting from the United States and others. The gunmen believed they were carrying out their holy duty to remove infidels from the planet. They believed that anyone who didn't accept their version of the Muslim faith was an infidel. Jews, Americans, Britons, and others are particularly disgusting to these killers, and they're eliminated without hesitation. Is this evil?

Teach Only Love

The *Course in Miracles,* published by the Foundation for Inner Peace, teaches that the only error humans can commit is that of separation. That is, when humankind thinks of itself as separate from God, from creation, and from fellow human beings, then the error is made. The lesson: *teach only love!*[1]

Where is the reconciliation? Dying to the physical is something we all must do, but is it something we should all accept as necessary if we're confronted as the rabbi and others were? That's exactly what took place in Mumbai in November 2008.

America is a nation built on individuality that takes pride in self-sufficiency. Many Eastern ideas suggest that merging oneself with the One is the way out, the escape from the wheel of rebirth, the great illusions—known as *Maya*. But the problem of evil is a real sticking point. How do we accept that we're one with all, one with the bad guy, and still act responsibly in our world? Right action insists on protecting the innocent, doesn't it?

Right Action

What should the world do when there are massacres in such places as Darfur? Is it responsible to intervene to save the innocent? There's a saying that the military really gets: "Freedom isn't free!" I suggest that peace isn't free, either.

Is it true that force begets force? When in history has noninterference and carte blanche permissiveness—an "anything goes" philosophy—ever led to peace? The fact is, there has been no such time.

As confusing as it might seem, freedom requires responsible action—not the inaction that puts its head in the sand and argues: "There's no evil in the world!" The sacred texts of every religion contain stories of moral conflict. In all of them, good must battle the so-called evil in the world in order for peace to be achieved. There's a paradox here, for the peace that comes from practicing teachings that encourage allowing, accepting, and turning everything over to the divine is undeniable. Still, are these lessons fundamentally about peace or escapism?

Peace or Escapism?

During the years that my work was all about catching the "bad guy," I often struggled with this polarity. Unconditional love isn't unconditional acceptance. Ancient documents from around the world for at least the past 3,000-plus years have pitted good against evil. In other words, at least from the perspective taught by spiritual leaders, there is wickedness on Earth (or there was at one point). At the same time, we're faced with temptation and other tests that will in some way demonstrate our worthiness to be saved or to escape rebirth and so forth, depending on the religious system we come from. We are also told that we're loved, cherished, innocent, and capable of doing godlike things.

In Christianity, for example, Jesus informs us that the kingdom of heaven is within and that all that he did, we can do—and more. Further, he insists that we're his brothers and sisters. In Hinduism, the process known as life is all about a special kind of realization, knowing that we are all one in the One. For the Hindus, our rectified self is like the stream merging with the sea, and in that sense losing its individual name. In other words, many of the things we Westerners hold on to and work to develop—such as self-esteem, ego identification, separation, distinction, and the like—are exactly what others seek to lose.

Additionally, Hindus have a caste system that declares some to be unclean. Should an unclean person even accidentally hear something from such sacred documents as the Upanishads, horrible things await him. Indeed, some have actually had molten lead poured into their ears. So we see that the two polarities are real, both explicitly and implicitly.

Living above the Fray

Some people now wish to say that evil no longer exists except in the mind. Remove it from our thoughts and it will cease to exist, at least in the world of those who hold no evil. Okay, let's look at this seriously. Chopra told Hannity of four teenagers with a gun whom he talked out of robbing and assaulting him—at least that's what he led the audience to assume. He would have the individual mind merge with the One mind and thereby ignore other minds. Note the operative word—*ignore*. For you see, four young men with at least one gun were intent on doing Chopra harm but were persuaded to do otherwise.

Does that mean the four now faithfully follow Chopra as students devoted to their guru? I doubt it. It probably means they assaulted someone else later. Forgive me if this offends you, but the law-enforcement side of me says it's good that Chopra was successful in negotiating his free passage; yet in failing to recognize the presence of evil, he released four individuals to harm someone else. If Chopra had then used his cell phone to report the incident so that the local authorities could pick up the teens or at least identify them, then he'd be admitting that there's evil in his world.

I do believe that people whose consciousness is above the fray—those who have a certain degree of innocence and peace, a presence that suggests they may actually have spoken to God, a sincere and earnest enthusiasm for higher worlds—can and do walk in dangerous situations without harm. I'm reminded, for example, of the hostage Ashley Smith in Atlanta who presented the teachings of *The Purpose Driven Life* to Brian Nichols, who held her captive. Nichols was on trial for rape when he shot and killed the presiding judge, shot and killed the court reporter, and then shot and killed a deputy as he fled the courthouse. He then killed a federal agent as he escaped, before taking Smith hostage. It was reported that Nichols decided to turn himself in after hearing part of *The Purpose Driven Life* read to him by Smith. The book is by the minister Rick Warren, and its teachings certainly don't dismiss the presence of evil. Rather, like many Christian books, it offers the hope of redemption.

The Magnet of the Mind

Although my experience leads me to dismiss the notion that there's no evil in the world, at the same time I believe that the mind can and does create an environment that can attract or repel, like a magnet, the experiences and environment one has. As a young child, I was often bullied. I was tall and skinny for my age and also timid. The timidity attracted the bullies, for they saw someone easily frightened. I'll spare you the entire story, but by the time I was in the fifth grade, I'd had enough of being bullied and hiding it from my father, who would have had nothing to do with a son who was a coward. I therefore stood up and fought. I beat up the bully, and that started a string of fights that lasted until my senior year in high school.

As I look back on this, I can see more clearly what really happened. I was tired of being picked on, so I began visualizing myself beating the bullies at their own game. Every night when I went to bed, I pictured myself fighting, seeing it so vividly that I moved in the bed as my right fist followed a couple of left jabs, and so forth. I know now that this neuromuscular training, as professionals call it today, provided me with skill and ability, and the creative visualization attracted the opportunities to show my stuff.

This may have aided me in getting even, but it also seriously interfered with many real opportunities, including such things as college scholarships. The visualization process is a magnet of sorts, and whether it's the observer interacting with the observed, a function of physics, or a matter of self-fulfilling prophecy, the difference is truly academic.

Another experience shows the positive aspects of the envisioning process. I lived in California during a major earthquake, but I had made it a practice to mentally surround my house with light each night at bedtime. The earthquake damaged neighbors' properties on all sides of me, but not my home. In fact, my wife and I slept through the entire thing, and reportedly no sober person could have done so. I don't have the answer as to why this happened, only my strong suspicion that the practice of surrounding my home with protective white light had something to do with it all. So could giving up the idea of evil actually end evil, or would it just eliminate me from being on the receiving end and leave the evil free to go attack my innocent neighbors?

Wishful Thinking

If I look closely at the lessons of those who teach peace, to turn the other cheek, and nonviolent resistance, they all indicate that there's something to resist. The yin and yang of life, the light and the dark, the male and the female, the good and the bad—all are the opposites that make the whole. As many teachers have shared with us, perhaps evil is necessary for us to know good just as we need dark to appreciate light. With that said, I do still believe somehow, down deep within myself, that if enough light is shed on a situation, not the slightest of shadows can remain.

The world today is a very poor reflection of the highest aspects of humanity. I do believe in those higher qualities, and I do think one day all of the evil can be rectified. I do not, however, believe that this will happen by or through denial. If I'm to live a truly illuminated life, I first have to step out of the world so I can live in it but not of it. Therein is the key—in it but not of it. What does that mean?

If I live truly from the spirit, and therefore not from the world, I should transcend the so-called evils that somehow still seem to have claimed the lives of so many great and wise leaders of the past from all traditions, including Jesus of Nazareth. But since that doesn't appear to be the case (evil does not disappear), is there really any reason to believe that this world would still exist without its opposites? Is it only fanciful wishing to believe so? Even so, is it still not worth striving for? What does that say about us? And what does that mean?

✧✧✧ ✧✧✧

chapter 18

THE STRUGGLE TO FORGIVE

"Integrity without knowledge is weak and useless, and knowledge without integrity is dangerous and dreadful."
— Samuel Johnson

Years ago I read a marvelous book entitled *Teach Only Love,* by Gerald G. Jampolsky, M.D. It impressed me a great deal, so much so that I went on to read all of Jampolsky's books. Some of his words echo in my head to this day. One of those insistent reverberations is: "We teach what we want to learn."

You may know that my real career change from criminalist to what I do today occurred largely as the result of research I carried out with two others in a prison system. There I discovered the power of forgiveness to rehabilitate even the hardest of the hard. The real power in forgiveness comes from surrendering blame. As long as we blame, we effectively neutralize our ability to empower ourselves. It displaces responsibility, and that leads us into the victim role—truly an emotionally circular, inward-spiraling quagmire.

Nothing changes unless we do, and blame prohibits any transformation. The evidence for this is overwhelming, despite it seeming somewhat counterintuitive, given our "it's okay to get even" culture . In my book *Choices and Illusions,* I amply covered that evidence and the tentacles that arrest us when we blame. So for the moment, I'll just ask you to take this at face value: blame is bad, forgiveness undoes blame, and that's good.

Remember: "We teach what we want to learn." I've always believed that life is for lessons. We have opportunities to learn certain things, and if we don't do so the first time, another teacher brings a new, tougher challenge and gives us another chance. In other words, I believe, based on my experience, that each time the lesson comes back, it's more difficult than before. The moral is obvious—learn quickly, hopefully the first time around.

Releasing Blame

Sometimes I think of those things for which I still have strong negative feelings that are wrapped in some angst, and I work to let them go. I find the most difficult those that involve injury not to myself, but to another, especially if it's someone I care for. It's as if the violation of a loved one is much more difficult to accept than injury to ourselves. It's clear to me that after so many years of teaching forgiveness, I'm still learning what I teach.

I regularly release those feelings of anger or disgust toward all whom I still mentally hold accountable for something—and I bless them as well. Allowing myself to recognize these emotions within me tends to release them, whereas attempting to drown them out is only denial. I've personally experienced the power that comes from releasing blame and forgiving, despite the fact that in some rare instances the task has been daunting.

For example, a scoutmaster once pulled what in law enforcement we call a switcheroo on my son, taking his beret from his head on the pretense that he was adjusting it, but then giving it to another young man because it would fit that boy better. My son had had his name written in the beret and then received it as part of his Cub Scout Arrow of Light ceremony (something parents pay for but the troop hands out). When my son discovered this action, his eyes filled with tears. I was sitting nearby when the switcheroo happened, but I was in a conversation with another parent and not watching the incident, about 20 feet away. It took several minutes after the meeting for me to get the details of what had happened from my tearful son. He'd trusted his Scout leader—aren't you supposed to?

Two adult assistants were nearby, and I knew one of them. Addressing him, I finally got the truth. Not only had it happened as my son had said, but the man knew it had happened, although he denied it at first. I was furious. There was a promise that in the next meeting my son would receive an apology and his beret would be returned. The fact is that the scoutmaster himself saw no harm and refused to apologize, stating about my son (and I quote): "He's not the kind of boy that would like Scouts anyway."

What's a parent to do? I was a Boy Scout when I was a young, and I could trust my scoutmaster. What had changed? I wrote to the local council of the Boy Scouts of America, but they didn't respond. I spoke with other adults, and although they condemned the action, they said that they were powerless to do anything. Sometimes I still think of this situation and realize that this child and his younger brother both missed Scouting in their lives because of this one infantile would-be leader. If I'd been dishonest, I could have claimed there was a $100 bill hidden in the hat, and insisted on the return of the money, but I couldn't compound the problem by telling a lie.

Forgiving this and letting it go remains a challenge, and I believe much more so because the injury was to someone I care for rather than myself. Why is it easier to forgive someone who injures you as opposed to a loved one?

Natural Wiring

It's natural to think of ways to get even when we're hurt. We come into this world wired for some things. That doesn't mean permanently set, only prewired. Research shows us, for example, that newborn

133

rhesus monkeys have cells in the auditory portions of their brains that respond in full fashion when a rhesus call of alarm is enunciated. They somehow know this call at birth, without ever hearing it before, so there has been no operant conditioning whatsoever. That kind of prewiring can predispose us, but it can also be extinguished. The question might be: should it?

It's said that things happen for a reason. Some would step forward upon hearing my son's Scouting story and with conviction attempt to persuade me that it was for the best. Perhaps they'd point out events that might have occurred had he remained in Scouts. They could remind me that the reason I pulled both boys from Scouting was that the careless disregard and dishonest dealings of the leader were excused because they took place with a juvenile. There probably are things about the organization that my son was saved from, and the optimistic view is to think of those things. Perhaps I had so much fun and learned so much from Scouting that I get fixated on what he lost, when I should be focused on what he may have gained instead. After all, this was hardly a real disaster, was it?

What Happened Was Supposed to Happen

Think of those who lost loved ones in the attacks of 9/11. Do you think the survivors get comfort out of believing that what happened was supposed to happen? Some may, I'm sure. Comfort is exactly what this form of thinking provides, and there's nothing wrong with that until we extend it everywhere. In science, there are laws. Typically, they give rise to predictability and apply in all situations, or they aren't laws. Even with Newtonian physics, the law of gravity says that gravity pulls something toward the center of the earth and does so reliably according to the rule (directly proportional to the mass and indirectly proportional to the distance separating the two masses), unless certain circumstances known in the world of quantum physics are present.

What, then, do you think of a law that suggests that everything happens for a reason, if that means *everything?* Consider the Holocaust, the genocide in Rwanda, the burning of witches, the Ku Klux Klan's heinous acts, and so on. There's no shortage of appalling tragedies perpetrated by humans, but if they were all supposed to happen, then should we resign ourselves to believing: "What will be, will be"? I think not.

There's injustice in the world, and as agents capable of acting, we should do something. Our action can be noble or ignoble—we choose—but even inaction is activity in the sense that it's a choice. When is it okay to allow an injustice to go unchallenged?

A Reality Check

All creation epics tell stories of the conflict between good and evil. The Judeo-Christian and Zoroastrian view in particular has a battle between the hosts of heaven. The struggle between good and evil is archetypal, so it may be comforting to think that everything happens for some reason. Maybe it does, but I'm compelled to include this as a principle behind that premise: the need to act in a manner that supports the dignity of innocence and the rights we have in our society that are safeguarded by law. Remember that even if "everything is as it's supposed to be," you're there as an observer, and you have a choice about how to respond. Do you simply ignore a crime, watch an innocent person being injured while you look on, or do you get involved? What do you think? And what does that mean, anyway?

As we've discussed, everything that stinks may just stink—there may be no redeeming value per se, there may just be bad folks with evil intent or careless people who are morally and spiritually asleep to their true possibility. That doesn't mean we should give up or stop holding out for a better world. It just means that we recognize some cold, hard facts. I prefer to be an optimist, but to temper my positive outlook with a reality check from time to time. I'm certain that one day I'll no longer hold thoughts of getting even—I'll find a way to forgive. What about you?

✧✧✧ ✧✧✧

chapter 19

THE STILL, SMALL
VOICE WITHIN

*"There is no witness so dreadful, no accuser so terrible as
the conscience that dwells in the heart of every man."*
— Polybius

I was raised to believe that there was an inner voice that would guide each one of us, and it was thought of as a person's conscience. It was this voice that would prod us away from temptation and toward the spiritually correct. That inner voice would guide, but I don't remember anyone telling me that it would audibly speak to me. Yet, although I've never literally *heard* the inner voice speak to me per se, I've had such strong mental impressions that it was as though I were being spoken to silently. For me, hearing this internal guidance is a matter of processing an impression that's sometimes emotional but usually semantic, but it isn't as though someone is talking to me via sound waves.

Inner Guidance

The first time I remember processing (hearing) an inner voice was when I lost my taw marble. I listened to the voice tell me where to

137

step, followed the instructions faithfully, and found the marble lying at my feet. Since then, I've had dialogues with some part of me, some voice within, on many occasions. I believe we all do this to some extent, but how reliable is this inner counsel?

When I made the solitary journey to the desert that I mentioned earlier, I was told to take an amethyst in a copper mount, strung on a gold chain. I was also told that I'd obtain this amethyst and chain from a lapidary (an artisan who works with minerals and gemstones) in Las Vegas, Nevada. I checked all the stores, and when I finally went to the last one, they told me—as had the others—that they didn't have such a thing. I joked, "But I was told you did—you know, in a meditation." The woman at the counter then asked me to wait a minute, and she went into the back room. She returned with the owner, who opened a small brown envelope and removed a copper-mounted amethyst. The gold chain was easy to locate, and I left the store with exactly what I'd been told I would find.

The thought keeps creeping in as I write that some will dismiss this book as deluded. So be it, if that's the case. I can only share with you the truth as I know it, and I've repeatedly relied on this inner guidance for a variety of matters.

One day a couple of investigators who worked for me were searching the garbage in a large Dumpster while I sorted recovered papers of interest. As I worked, a small handwritten memo came into view. There was no way of confirming right then that this document contained the name and phone number of the party we were seeking to connect to the owner of the garbage. As I started to dismiss the item and let it fall back into the trash, I was told by some internal wisdom: *This is the paper you're looking for.* I held on to the memo and stopped the search right then and there. It turned out to be exactly what we were seeking.

On another occasion, I remember hurting my back and finally, after living with it for some time, asking for guidance. I was told *Ginseng* in a dream that night, and sure enough, when I made the ginseng mixture as I'd seen in the dream, the pain ended and stayed away.

I also recall some of my early attempts at astral projection. I was concerned about the stories I'd heard about many problems that could arise while out of the body. I asked for inner guidance and was informed that I'd be looked after, so I went ahead and experienced my first voluntary journey. However, my partner awoke in the middle of that night, startled to find a face staring at the bed from where the ceiling met the wall. She told me of this the next day, but explained that she'd felt safe and that I'd know what it was, so she went back to sleep. A couple of weeks later, she brought the Sunday paper to me to show me the face. It was the same, she claimed, as a mask from an ancient culture.

Many times in my life this inner impression, this inner voice, has led me to announce the sex of unborn children, foretell marriages, and do other such things. I even believe that I've understood animal communication in the same way, and further, that the animals have understood me. That said, you might ask if I believe in these inner communications, and my answer would be: "Sometimes yes, and sometimes no." Why is that?

The Law of Self-Exemption

Years ago while attending a physical-security school, I listened to a tangential remark about cigarette smoking. The lecturer, making a comparison to a lack of security, asserted that those who smoke are employing the psychological law of self-exemption. I'd never encountered this theory in my psychology studies and failed to find it when I checked in the *Dictionary of Psychology*. Nonetheless, I immediately related to the implicit nature of this law—the idea that consequences will befall everyone but oneself.

I was a heavy smoker for 44 years. For most of that time, I smoked between two and three packs of cigarettes a day. I began when everyone had this habit. I used to watch Edgar R. Murrow and Walter Cronkite presenting the evening news, each with a lighted cigarette in the ashtray that sat conspicuously on the desk in front of them. I watched physicians give testimonials about the best and the healthiest cigarettes.

As time went by, I witnessed, as did many, a complete about-face with respect to smokers and smoking. When my youngest son, aged seven at the time, informed me that he was going to smoke when he grew up unless I stopped, I quit. I turned my attention to every detail involving cigarette consumption and asked my higher self for help. I went to bed that night in April 2006 knowing, assured by the small voice inside, that when I arose the next morning I'd be a nonsmoker. Before receiving my son's encouragement—if that's what you choose to call his loving form of blackmail—I practiced the psychological law of self-exemption. I convinced myself that, similar to something Jesus said and paraphrased by me: "It's not what one puts in his mouth that will be his undoing; rather, it's what comes out of his mouth."

I knew fully the power of belief and refused to believe that smoking would injure my health. I often asked my inner voice if I had this right, and I was always assured that I did. I even lectured about how wrong health-care providers were when they insisted that smoking was always a death sentence. I often pointed out just how powerful this influence could be. Sometimes I cited a cancer study that I'd conducted in which every patient whose physician didn't believe that the mind had a role in healing died during the course of the study, whereas everyone who believed in the power of the mind in wellness and whose physician encouraged this lived. Every member of this latter group was in remission three years following the study.

Three Special Beings

In the early 1990s, I was scheduled to speak at a conference featuring continuing education for psycho- and hypnotherapists. Although I arrived too late the night before my session to attend the banquet, I heard that a woman who'd worked for years for the hypnosis school that was sponsoring the conference lit a cigarette after eating. One of the doctors in the front row had stepped up and taken her cigarette, stubbed it out in the ashtray, and publicly scolded her. I was astonished by his audacity and infuriated by his rudeness, so

I adjusted my presentation accordingly. I opened my speech with an imaginary tale, saying something like this:

"I want you all to imagine that there are three very special beings on their way to this conference right now. They've heard of all the fine healers who are attending, so they've come from vast distances and across time itself just to join us, to share and learn from us. One of them is the Buddha of India, one is Jesus of Nazareth, and the last is Edgar Cayce. Now you all know who Buddha and Jesus are, and I suspect that most of you are familiar with Cayce, but just to be certain, I'll tell you that he's considered the father of holistic medicine. He gave thousands of readings to the ill while in an altered state of consciousness, a self-induced hypnosis. His documented success is absolutely astonishing.

"So, we have three special people arriving, and I suggest something like this will happen. One-third of you may run to Cayce, the chain-smoker, and tell him how you can help him stop smoking. Another third may have a weight-loss regimen ready for Buddha. Perhaps the remaining third know how to help Jesus keep kosher.

"To be a healer doesn't mean insulting and otherwise injuring an individual by self-righteous actions. I remind you that what we heal today—the so-called causes of humankind's woes—aren't always the culprits of tomorrow. Where yesterday we spoke harshly about liquor, today we learn that a glass of wine in the evening has numerous health benefits, and so forth."

I continued, but the point I intended to make remains the same: the words of the healer are as powerful as any other tool he or she can use.

For me, the matter was at least partially one of belief. Whenever I heard or saw a cigarette commercial that warned against smoking, I mentally cancelled the message in my head and often changed the station. I did all of this just to preserve in my mind and belief the sanctity of smoking.

Meeting Jesus

One day I visited my dentist. I'd just changed providers because of a bad experience with my previous dentist. He'd left a broken drill bit inside a root canal, where it had become infected and given me grief on and off for a couple of years. My new dentist had his new son-in-law, also a dentist, working that day, so I saw the son-in-law. I was there for a minor filling—a simple process, except that the syringe wasn't aspirated and his aim wasn't that good. The injection, which contained epinephrine, went straight to my bloodstream. I felt my pulse racing, and by evening it seemed that my entire body was shaking with every beat of my pounding heart. My face was swelling, and I found myself in the emergency room dealing with what I thought was an allergic response to the injection.

I was treated for an allergic reaction and sent up to the cardio unit for more testing. They informed me of an irregular and rapid heartbeat, indicated that one side of the heart wasn't working as well as the other, gave me some blood-pressure medicine, and sent me on my way. Don't get me wrong—they were very professional about it, but also rather matter of fact. It was "no big deal" kind of stuff.

I went home, where I became very aware of every tiny difference in how my heart beat and how it felt in my chest. I awoke several nights in a row from a sound sleep with what felt like a large gas bubble in my chest. I finally decided to heal the whole thing myself by calling on the divine intelligence within. I did so over several evenings, and then one night I had a special dream. In the dream, I was lying on my bed, just as I usually slept, when Jesus came to my bedside, laid his hand on my leg, and told me, "Your heart is healed." I believe this was a dream, even though it seemed very real at the time and is still so real in my mind today that it's as clear as other events that actually happened.

I awakened the next morning, felt great, and went on enjoying myself, exercising daily on a bicycle or treadmill, biking or walking outdoors whenever the weather allowed. I continued in this manner for the next year or two.

I live in Washington state, over in the corner where Montana, Idaho, and Canada are all just an hour or two away. In this region, we get extreme weather. A couple of years after my dream, when spring finally came after a long winter, it was a welcome relief, and I couldn't wait to get outside and do something. I have a small hobby ranch on the outskirts of Spokane where my sons have had their horses, sheep, goats, rabbits, pigeons, chickens, doves, llamas, and so forth. There's always plenty to repair—"hot" wire to restring from deer jumping over it and dragging their legs into the lines, insulators to pull from the fence posts, welded wire to restretch, and more—as well as plenty to clean up. Come spring, instead of thinking of this as a chore, it's my escape, and I really look forward to getting back outdoors.

More Guidance

That particular spring, however, held a surprise for me. When I first started working outside, I felt a burning sensation in my chest. I thought it was in my left lung, and I attributed it to an allergy or something similar, something new that I'd never experienced. I'd never had an allergy or allergic reaction before the dental incident, but after that event I'd become alert to other factors that might negatively affect me in some way. I reported the feeling to my wife but also noted that when I kept on going, it simply disappeared. In other words, I could work right through it, so I did. I did so over and over again for more than a month, until one day when Ravinder was outside with me and the burning sensation came on as we were working together. I told her about it again, and she asked for more details. She then said that it sounded like a very strange allergy and that I should have it checked out.

The following morning, she had tears in her eyes when she came out to where I was. While preparing her morning cup of tea, she'd glanced at the back of a cereal box on the shelf above the mugs. On that box was the description of my symptoms, and they weren't associated with any allergy—rather, they were the warning signs of an impending heart attack. I reassured her and agreed to go in for testing as soon as I could.

I saw my doctor that very day and he scheduled me for a nuclear stress test the following Friday. But that wasn't just any old Friday—no, my test was scheduled for Friday the 13th. I told myself going to the test that 13 was a lucky number, really. Think of it—13 colonies were the start of this great country.

After the nuclear scan, I watched the EEG chart as I ran on the treadmill, and when the two nurses conducting the exam stopped me, I pointed out the irregular patterns. They didn't comment, only smiled and informed me that my physician would let me know the results.

My cell phone rang less than two hours later. I was to return on Monday for an angiogram. I was to be prepared for the possibility that I might stay overnight, but I probably wouldn't. On Monday when the procedure began, my consciousness melted away under the anesthesia. When my eyes opened again, I saw my wife sobbing with our younger son by her side. She informed me that triple-bypass surgery was the recommendation. Two of the three main arteries to my heart were completely blocked and one was 99 percent blocked. I was told that cardiologists refer to this condition as the "widow maker"! I was lucky to be there.

I'd asked my inner guide about this condition and repeatedly been assured that I'd be okay. Triple-bypass surgery didn't fit my definition of okay! The good news was that my heart was fine. Somehow it had found ways to get blood to all of its parts, building its own bypasses, and so the organ itself was perfectly healthy. There was no damage at all!

I thought of the dream in which Jesus healed my heart. I was grateful, but if that had been real, why not my arteries as well?

In April 2007, I had triple-bypass surgery. The procedure went off without a problem, other than the difficulty the anesthesiologist encountered with inserting the breathing tube. I was remarkably calm about it all. Somehow I knew that if it was my time, it was my time, so I turned it all over. That's really just what I did.

My wife told me later that she went home after the surgery rather than staying in my room because she saw spiritual beings surrounding me, taking care of me. I, too, sensed them. When I awoke, Ravinder and my sons were there to hold my hand, and I assured them I was fine.

I was in good humor when I regained consciousness, laughing and joking with the nurse in intensive care because she wouldn't give me water. I promised my youngest son that I'd be home by the weekend. I regained consciousness from the surgery on Wednesday evening around 9 P.M. and went home Sunday morning around 9 A.M. Thursday, Friday, and Saturday were sobering days. It was only then that I really learned the truth about what I'd undergone.

What Open-Heart Surgery Really Means

You may know that during open-heart surgery, they not only cut you in two and pull your chest apart so that the surgeon can get his or her hands into it, but they also take your heart out of the equation by means of bypass pumps and send your blood through a warmer while the procedure goes on. Unfortunately, this warming process generates microembolisms that negatively affect memory. So the "afterlife," if you will, includes not only the physical healing but also the relearning process involved in attempting to regain certain memories. My initial reaction upon discovering this wasn't positive at all.

I was feeling sorry for myself after the surgery. I found myself angry at that internal voice, which had always been right in the past. I felt betrayed, but I didn't know for sure why or how, because I also knew that I was okay and that I'd been taken care of. As time went on, I found that I felt healthier and healthier until one day, when a nurse asked me about the surgery, I told her that it was like an internal Botox—I just felt younger in every way. (Never mind this fact that I chose not to share with her: the pectoral muscles end up looking like feminine breasts because they've been separated down the middle in order to open the chest!)

My recovery was fast, and those around me—including new people I've met since the operation—all insist they can't tell that I ever had open-heart surgery. I continue to exercise every day. My health-care professionals tell me the problem was cholesterol and genetic in origin, so I watch my diet, pop the daily dose of prescription meds, and direct my internal higher self to heal me in every way, every day.

Still, a change happened in that period that took something away from me. I didn't speak to or trust the inner voice at all for months. Today I listen, but I moderate carefully, and I don't always fully rely on what I hear. It's hard to think that this internal guidance could be right on so many occasions for so long and then be so wrong regarding my heart. Did I misunderstand, or did I just tell myself what I wanted to hear and put the blame on that still, small voice within?

Be Careful What You Wish For

At the time of the surgery, I'd reconciled myself to passing on, if that was the will of God. My greatest desire to remain was for my family. I'd always thought I wanted to pass in my early 60s, before age took a heavy toll. I knew of Edgar Cayce as the chain-smoking sleeping prophet who told his wife that he was tired and just chose to pass over before he got any older. He died about one hour before I was born. My wife is convinced that not only had I planned—albeit subconsciously—to do something similar, but that I'd actually set it all up.

Then I changed my mind. I had two young sons and a different life from the one I had when I originally made these plans, and it was the open-heart surgery that restarted everything for me. Is that possible? Intuitively, I believe so. Still, something pulls at my trust of this inner voice. Should it? Does it matter? Do *you* trust your inner voice?

chapter 20

INTUITION AND THE SELF-PSYCHIC

"I feel there are two people inside me—me and my intuition. If I go against her, she'll screw me every time, and if I follow her, we get along quite nicely."
— **Kim Basinger**

The still, small voice within and intuition—how do they differ? When we have a hunch or a strong feeling, when we're urged by something inside to move toward or away from a decision—are we not talking about one and the same thing? The still, small voice, the conscience, intuition, even the so-called inner psychic, aren't they just different aspects of the same inner-guidance system? Where does this come from?

Some believe that this phenomenon originates from a spiritual plane, whereas others insist that it's only a throwback to the prehistoric days of the bicameral mind—a time when we all heard voices inside, a time when oracles really spoke, at least within our own heads.[1] Scholars don't agree that there ever was a so-called bicameral time in that sense; and religious leaders, mystics, and magi fail to agree on the source as well. For most of them, sometimes the voice comes from within and sometimes from without. Prophecy, after all, presupposes the inherent right of the gods to address humankind.

As children, most of us generally have an imaginary friend or friends. There comes a time when we leave these friends behind. In other words, we outgrow them or our need for them. Should we also move beyond our relationship with the guidance from within?

It's altogether too easy for people to claim to know something and really know very little at all. Most of us believe that we understand why we make decisions, and yet even when they turn out to be wrong, we still believe we know why we made those choices. Thus, when politicians who oppose a war are asked why they voted for it in the first place, they have an answer: faulty intelligence. Not all decisions, however, are based on anything other than faulty consciousness—faulty in the sense that we think the conscious mind made the call when indeed it was actually decided upon by the subconscious.[2]

Subconscious Biases

We all have biases, many of them hidden from us. For instance, Jesse Jackson admitted, to his embarrassment, that when he heard footsteps approaching from behind on a dark night and he turned and saw a white man, he was relieved. He was admitting a subconscious bias that he had just become aware of. Again, all of us have these unconscious views. The bias can be racial or intellectual; or relate to authority, age, gender, nationality, language, and on and on. In fact, it's fair to ask whether it's reasonable *not* to have any biases. After all, favoring the advice of a wealthy person over that of a poor person might assist us in making more money. But how about living happily? A preference in favor of the wisdom of the elderly over that of a six-year-old is probably helpful—unless the subject is music and the six-year-old is Bach.

So when is a bias a good thing?

Original Thoughts

That stream of inner talk that constantly goes through our heads also has a bias—indeed, it has many. If I listen to it all the time, am I not just reinforcing them? Is there some breakthrough that can be triggered or actuated in some way so that creativity suddenly follows?

How many original thoughts have you had today? How many do you have in a week? Does everyone just rethink what someone else has come up with somewhere else at some other time? Original thought—what is that, anyway?

When the voice within gives me a new idea, can I rely on that more than on the same old, same old? Original thought consists of two types for our purposes here. The first is truly original: no one else (or practically no one) has put these concepts together. The second can be said to be the creativity that one may bring to ideas that are already in existence. The two kinds are rarely completely separate. Take the creative work of J. K. Rowling, author of the Harry Potter series. In 2007, she earned more than $300 million from her creative works. In third place for earnings was the horror writer Stephen King with $45 million. It would appear that truly creative, original thinking has a big payday in it. How many of us venture into the mental realm that underlies such success stories?

If creativity and originality are the only criteria by which I can trust my inner voice, then I'm in trouble, for there are plenty of so-called original thoughts routinely shared in psychiatric wards between patients—certainly that sort of originality isn't what we seek. How then do we know when to trust our inner guidance?

How do we know when to listen to anyone about anything? If we ask our spouse how we look, we expect a biased reply. The closer someone is to us, the more inclined that person is to give us the answer we want, to reassure us. When we talk to ourselves, we can expect strong biases, some of which can be anticipated and some of which can't. The hidden ones may announce themselves in the same startling way Jesse Jackson reported experiencing, but they're unknown until they do. And because these tendencies exist in everyone, the information we get from any source can be shaped by unknown forces.

Informed and Aware

The long and the short of it for me comes down to this: we listen, but we question; and we suspend judgment, doing our best to make a fully informed and aware choice. Informed and aware simply means that we're sensitive to our limitations, the nature of bias itself, and the many nuances that have programmed the alternatives that we might choose from in the first place.

Choice has been thought of as an illusion and in my book on the topic, *Choices and Illusions,* a good deal of paper is used to illustrate just how true that can be. Here, however, let me simply point out two elements that we need to safeguard rigorously.

The first is our attitude toward what we call knowledge. We can think that we know something, such as $1 + 1 = 2$, and then find out that one gallon of alcohol added to one gallon of water doesn't equal two gallons. Our knowledge should always be examined in context, even though we've been taught quite the opposite.

Second, it's our prerogative to be alert to alternatives. Only we can decide when we've explored all possibilities. Knee-jerk reactions rob us of thought. Becoming angry because we're cut off in traffic offers only a few options. Choosing to respond differently is a matter of redefining the context in which we see the stimuli. As we saw with the example of spit in the mouth and then putting spit in a glass, shifting the context changes everything.

Choosing to See Good

If I choose to see good in all, then I've altered the context for most of the troubling experiences that I might have in life. I truly do have the ability to decide to view everything as coming to me for some ultimate good, even if it isn't immediately obvious. Choosing to allow that perhaps the god within, that creative spark of divinity that created you and *is* you at some higher level, is sometimes coming through in your inner communications can clear matters up when it comes to what, when, and where one listens. For me, it's easy to see that my self-identification, complete with its ego functions, and my higher or quintessential self sometimes dialogue with each other and sometimes with themselves. The trickster, to use Carl Jung's schema,[3] often seems to mediate these inner discourses, akin to a court in which the judge appears to expose one side or the other but not necessarily on solid grounds. The result can be just what I heard regarding my heart surgery. I'm okay, indeed better in many ways. I was protected, in one manner of speaking, by not knowing what lay ahead long in advance. My heart is healthy, and no promise was broken. What that all means seems relative to who's asking and who's answering the question.

In years past, I played games with my knowledge and intuitive gifts. As such, it was easy for me to pretend to be psychic. With a little old-fashioned psychology, anyone can be psychic. Not truly psychic, like John Edward, host of the television shows *Crossing Over with John Edward* and *John Edward Cross Country,* or a handful of others who have willingly put their gifts on the table for science to verify, but psychic to the beholder of the moment. I might have used very similar tools in an interrogation but never called it being psychic, because it wasn't. Sometimes I've seen honest people begin to believe they're psychic and rationalize their errors while collecting payment for their services. What we choose to believe and believe *in* are a very large part of what discretion and life itself is all about. I admonish my children: be careful what you believe, but hold true to it if it serves your highest best interest, for the faith itself may be the creative force that interlaces reality with belief.

Does it really matter? What do you think?

chapter 21

ALTERED STATES

*"From the living fountain of instinct flows everything
that is creative; hence the unconscious is not merely
conditioned by history, but is the very source of the creative
impulse. It is like Nature herself—prodigiously
conservative, and yet transcending her own historical
conditions in her acts of creation."*
— **Carl Jung**

A lot of literature today deals with altered states of consciousness. Rapid eye movement (REM), meditation, hypnosis, self-hypnosis—or for that matter, watching television—all have one thing in common, and that's the altered brain-wave state. The meaning of *altered* here is simple. The normal, fully awake and alert brain-wave activity is known as beta and is typically between 15 and 30 cycles per second (CPS). In the altered state, brain-wave activity declines. Alpha is the name of the phase between 8 and 14 CPS; below that is theta, which ranges from 4 to 7 CPS. What we know about these altered states for certain is something that's referred to as "hyper-suggestibility."

Practical Metaphysics

Years ago, I sometimes taught weekend courses in practical metaphysics. There was at that time, as there still is, quite a bit of interest in reincarnation, astral projection, aura reading, and so forth. I used altered states, typically group hypnosis, to guide participants in their inquiries. One such exercise called for a series of steps in altered states, designed to lead participants back to their past lives. After the appropriate direction, preparation, and countdowns, I suggested that in a moment they'd be transferred to a memory of a past life.

Of course, I instructed them in such a way as to eliminate tragic or traumatic experiences, but I told them what I wanted them to look for. I might say something like this: "Be sure to notice the kind of furniture and the wood it's made of. Is the style Early American, French Provincial or something else? Be sure to note the state of technology or the lack thereof, the hairstyles, the clothing, and so on, for all of these represent clues that may help you remember more when you return to normal consciousness."

I did these exercises long before false-memory syndrome became a daily headline, with one child after another falsely accusing a parent of molestation. Indeed, a psychologist friend of mine had a case that appeared on the surface to be unfounded. When I pointed that out to her, she became quite upset with me. But it takes very little to innocently suggest something to a subject under hypnosis. I know this well, because I was trained in forensic hypnosis, and I used it regularly.

Forensic Hypnosis

In one case, a young man was in prison for the murder of his mother. I was asked to use hypnosis with him and then run a lie-detection test to verify his statements afterward. I explained that I couldn't do that because a false memory created under hypnosis could theoretically pass the truth test. So we ran the lie-detection test first to see if he'd committed the homicide, and when he passed that, I went on with hypnosis.

This young man had been drinking and using drugs on the night in question. He claimed he had no memory of what had happened until he got home and found his mother dead on her bed. She'd been brutally murdered and then sexually assaulted.

Under hypnosis, this young man was able to remember many things that took place on that evening, including information that, when independently verified, precluded his ability to have been at the crime scene at the time of the homicide. I testified before the judge when the new evidence was brought forward, and this young man was rightfully released from state prison. The reason for including this story here is to emphasize the need to avoid suggesting anything when someone is in an altered state of consciousness. The hypnotist in this position should say such things as: "Where are you?" and "What did you do next?"

I became suspicious of information gained under altered states when a suggestion led the subject. To say to someone who's hypnotized: "You will now return to a past life, and when you arrive, I want you to notice everything—the clothing, the furniture, and so forth," is suggesting the experience and thereby potentially contaminating the find.

The Ancient Chinese Gentleman

That said, I have been a part of extraordinary experiences. A woman came to me when her back surgeon referred her to me for pain control, and she was a very good hypnosis subject—what's called a somnambule. I saw her once a week, and the sessions worked very well for her. About the fourth week, as I began to count her back up into ordinary consciousness, she spoke, telling me that someone was there and wanted to speak with me. I had another appointment, so I told her that we could talk next week and counted her back.

The next week when she came in, she reminded me to allow time to speak with this gentleman. So when it was time to count her up, I paused and asked if the person who wished to speak to me was there. When I received an affirmative answer, I provided the go-ahead cue and out of her mouth came a language I'd never heard before. After regaining my bearings, I grabbed a cassette recorder and began recording what she said.

Following the session, I asked the client if she knew what she'd said. Her answer was a story that went something like this: There was a dynasty ruler whose forces were defeated. A trusted follower of this leader was given a sacred scroll to hide so that it wouldn't be destroyed. The man speaking to me through her was the one who'd hidden the scroll. The drawing my client provided once out of hypnosis was a map to where it was hidden—in the Great Wall in China.

I handed the recording to a friend who had language experts at the University of Utah listen to it. He was told that it was probably an ancient Chinese dialect that hadn't been spoken for hundreds of years. At that time, a trip to China was out of the question. After the Kissinger-Nixon China accords, however, my friend Jeffrey Chamber Hughes was making a journey there, so I entrusted him with the map. Unfortunately, he was unable to identify the area it represented or to travel to regions that might have held a clue.

My hypnosis client didn't speak Chinese, nor had she ever been exposed to the language. I have no reason to doubt her sincerity, even though neither the language tape nor the map proved anything with absolute certainty. Perhaps I should have pursued it more fully, but life moves on. I was immersed in issues for a few years around that time that required almost all of my time and energy. Today when I think of this event, I wonder why I didn't ask my client to do more hypnosis of this kind. Of course I know why: at that time, the guild I belonged to prohibited that sort of inquiry with hypnosis. Later I resigned from the guild for that reason.

So altered states may lead to information that we have no explanation for or about. What does that mean? Should we trust all of this information? Certainly not. Where do we draw the line so that we aren't just gullible guppies who will swallow anything? What do you think? What does that mean?

chapter 22

CIVILITY, HUMILITY, SOCIETY, AND GENETICS: FINDING BALANCE IN ALL

"Ask yourself not if this or that is expedient, but if it is right."
— **Alan Paton**

Whenever we ask for the real self to stand up, whenever we honestly reflect on the meaning of life, whenever we take an accounting of ourselves in an attempt to answer that age-old question "Who am I?" the nature of the being and society are immediately called into question. By *being*, I'm referring to the genetic composition, and by *society*, the environment in which we've grown up. This is the old question of nature versus nurture. It has even more relevance today than in the past, because we now know that some behaviors are positively correlated with genetics, including criminal actions.[1]

Karma and Dharma and Magnetic Influence

Mystics generally teach that bad karma explains why some people suffer as they do, and good karma explains why others seem to always have the proverbial rabbit's foot, since everything "breaks right" for them. Astrologers teach that planetary positions influence the field in which someone is born, and this imprints the individual in ways that offer predispositions and propensities both favorable and not so desirable. All religious institutions have within them some construct that offers insight about why there's a vast disparity in opportunities and the human condition itself. Jesus was asked this question about a deformed man: "Is this man punished for his sins or the sins of another?"

Is it possible that modern physics can explain astrology, as some believe, by showing that electromagnetic influence differs ever so slightly with every single hour of the day? Does the field in which a person is born influence his development, aptitudes, and predispositions? Is it possible that genetics explains the principles of dharma and karma, or is it that genetics and physics are now just the modern terms we use, based on our current knowledge, to explain away our insecurity that arises when we see the world as simply a random accident?

Religious literature is full of saviors, as we saw earlier. Miracles attend all of them in some way or another, often with great similarities that lead an intellectual to conclude that the entire matter is just a myth generated to console the immature. What else could it be? Is it possible that just as the stimulation of certain regions of the brain causes a deep religious experience, as a species we're somehow wired to believe in God, to invent stories that explain creation, and to worship what we can't understand—death?

The natural thing for us to do at a very early age is to think of our minds as somehow separate, somehow able to participate without our bodies in adventures during sleep, and thus somehow also able to survive even death. Do we find it necessary therefore to hold on to the idea that death has no real control over our inner self, the very part of us that's reading and thinking about this book right now?

Everyone dies. Not one of the religious leaders who was heralded as the Great One lives in the flesh today, or at least not as they did at the time they were the Buddha or the Christ or Mohammed. Dying to the flesh is indeed a powerful metaphor that has given rise to countless ascetic movements, self-mutilation practices, and other sometimes bizarre and obscene customs. So why do some people say things such as: "He lost his battle with cancer and died last night." What do you mean—lost what?

Losing the Fight

As I mentioned earlier, I remember hearing Fox broadcaster Megyn Kelly become upset over this metaphor when Tony Snow passed over in 2008. I thought, *Great. Now there are at least three of us who think this metaphor is nonsense* (Megyn, my wife, and me). Does it matter if people use this problematic expression? The fact is that it absolutely does. How an issue is characterized makes all the difference in how we think about it. If we refer to a struggle as a war, it takes on an entirely different dimension in our psyche than a so-called police action. If, for example, we think of taking an illegal drug as a mistake, then we view it very differently from something referred to as a crime. In the latter scenario, the drug user may end up labeled as a criminal, whereas in the former, the person just made an error in judgment.

Context Framing

Remember when Henry Hyde attacked Bill Clinton over his sexual escapade with Monica Lewinsky? People in glass houses just shouldn't throw stones. Soon the world learned of an affair that Hyde had had with a married mother of young children that resulted in her divorcing her husband. Hyde referred to his own action, when it was made public, as "a youthful indiscretion." True, he was slightly younger at the time of his affair than Clinton was when he was President, but Hyde was past his teenage years by a couple of decades. So how youthful was it? And although no one condones Clinton's actions, Hyde's led to the breakup of a family and the separation of a father from his children—yet it was simply an indiscretion?

Again, how we frame things matters greatly. Like context, the characterization can dictate how we think about something. When we learn science, we typically are taught the Newtonian model and little about the quantum, but the fact is that quantum theory simply defies the Newtonian view. Things we believed were absolutes aren't found to be true when we peer into the tiny world of the micro. In fact, we learn that waves behave like particles and particles like waves, according to how we observe them. We discover that separating the observer from the observed makes no sense at a quantum level.

In fact, we find out that mind isn't the only action at a distant or nonlocal event. According to Bell's theorem, two subatomic particles can be separated over any distance and still influence each other instantly.[2] This is similar to the two groups of cells described earlier, only here we're speaking about inorganic subatomic matter—or is there really any such thing as inorganic?

If matter is connected across any distance, separated by light years, is it possible that minds are connected in the same or similar manner? Indeed, isn't it probable?

When we look into the world, it's easy to find incivility, rudeness, selfishness, ruthless disregard for others, and so on. I heard a story a very long time ago about the struggle for food. It seems that one day, the mouth and hands met and decided to object over how much work they had to do to feed the stomach. They argued about how much each should be responsible for, and in the end they went on strike. The refusal to see the interconnected nature of their situation led to their own starvation. Is it possible that we're doing something very similar to this when we treat others with disdain or incivility—or worse, a heavy weapon?

Balance

Is it appropriate to remove cancer? Can we agree on what constitutes this illness? How about a cancer of the human condition? What if there's a serial killer who won't be taken alive, and law enforcement ends up killing that individual in a gunfight? Most would say that this is as necessary for our society as removing cancer from the skin before it destroys the entire body. If that's the case, how about the war on terror? If there are people intent on killing us—and there certainly are—do we have an obligation to protect the innocent by stopping the terrorists?

Balancing all these things is, in part, what life's about. During the years when I ran lie-detection tests almost daily, I found that it was too easy to sour on the human race—they were all liars. I heard a John McCain ad pointing out that although Barack Obama had signed an agreement accepting federal funds and thereby limiting the amount of money that could be spent on a campaign, Obama had backed out of it. Then I heard Obama in his 30-minute, multimillion-dollar infomercial promise the American people that he'll always tell them the truth. I asked myself: *What? Is the lie to McCain your only lie ever? Does that mean you're 99 percent truthful? How would you like your wife, Michelle, to be 99 percent faithful?*

Balance is difficult, and it takes being honest with ourselves to achieve anything close to it. I can have thoughts that I don't want anyone to know, but if I deny them internally, I only hide the truth from myself. Here we are again, faced with the fact that just trying to follow the injunction to "know thyself" is much more difficult than we might think.

Reframing

The Tao says: "To find peace is to fulfill one's destiny." It seems that peace, like liberty, is neither easy nor free. Balance is obviously a prerequisite to peace. It also seems that perhaps we should reframe how we characterize matters, at least in our own minds, so that we get a chance to be honest with ourselves.

Not long ago I received this example from a friend about how reframing something creates an entirely different picture, whether you agree with the result or not.

A Pastor with *Guts!*

Thought you might enjoy this interesting prayer given in Kansas at the opening session of their Senate. It seems prayer still upsets some people.

When minister Joe Wright (*not* Jeremiah Wright) was asked to open the new session of the Kansas Senate, everyone was expecting the usual generalities, but this is what they heard:

"Heavenly Father, we come before you today to ask your forgiveness and to seek your direction and guidance. We know Your word says, 'Woe to those who call evil good,' but that is exactly what we have done. We have lost our spiritual equilibrium and reversed our values. We have exploited the poor and called it the lottery. We have rewarded laziness and called it welfare. We have killed our unborn and called it choice. We have shot abortionists and called it justifiable. We have neglected to discipline our children and called it building self-esteem. We have abused power and called it politics. We have coveted our neighbor's possessions and called it ambition.

"We have polluted the air with profanity and pornography and called it freedom of expression. We have ridiculed the time-honored values of our forefathers and called it enlightenment. Search us, oh God, and know our hearts today; cleanse us from every sin and set us free. Amen!"

The response was immediate. A number of legislators walked out during the prayer in protest. In six short weeks, Central Christian Church, where the Rev. Joe Wright is pastor, logged more than 5,000 phone calls with only 47 of those calls responding negatively.

The church is now receiving international requests for copies of this prayer from India, Africa and Korea. Commentator Paul Harvey aired this prayer on his radio program, *The Rest of the Story.*

I'm definitely passing it on. If you happen to disagree with any of the minister's prayer, then you can see more easily than most just how reframing something changes people's feelings and how it's thought about. Often, it's our emotions that rule our minds. In fact, researchers are now beginning to demonstrate that thinking itself may only be the product of experience.

The Brain/Mind Circularity

Some artificial-intelligence researchers have turned the classical models of the mind upside down. Instead of thinking of the brain as building abstract models, these scientists are more and more convinced that the experience of its world builds the mind. Linda Smith of Indiana University, Bloomington, puts it this way: "It's really through the body and the dynamic coupling of neural systems for perception, action and introspection, that cognition emerges."[3]

So it seems that the mind simply isn't something that precedes and survives the organ brain. This also implies that not only will science be successful at building thinking robots, but our entire self-image as individuals and as a race may require rethinking.

Stop—let's ponder this together. First, thoughts I have are given to me by the subconscious, so I don't even know why I'm going to think what I do.[4] Second, the thinking system—the mind stuff—is the result of my organs interacting in their environment, so clearly my mind must have originated from experience. Therefore, the mind can't be a blank slate on which everything is written because it simply doesn't exist until the physical brain builds the slate to write on.

Does this reduce the human condition to an evolutionary step in a world of randomness? Are we closer to knowing more about ourselves if we understand that we're connected to everything just as two particles in Bell's theorem?[5] Or have we lost something if we discover with certainty that mind didn't exist before the brain built it? Balance—where's the balance? Does it matter?

I suspect not, if finding ourselves isn't part of why we live. Can we use this information to learn to be caring and civil? Can we find balance in a world so apparently off-kilter? Or is it our perception that makes the world what it is, like observing matter as a wave because we choose to, or conversely, observing matter as a particle, again because we choose to?

163

chapter 23

THE BIG GIVE

"A hungry man is not free."
— attributed to **Adlai Stevenson**

Pay It Forward is a book written by Catherine Ryan Hyde that was made into a movie of the same name, starring Kevin Spacey, Helen Hunt, and Haley Joel Osment. The movie tells of a young boy who attempts to improve the world by aiding others in a novel way. Instead of repaying people for their favors, the idea is to pay it forward by doing a favor for someone else. This simple idea, based on a boy's belief in the goodness of human nature, has sparked similar efforts throughout America. There are even organizations such as The Pay It Forward Foundation that promote the idea, and Oprah Winfrey used her television show to run a popular series on the subject that helped many people. However, Oprah used the concept in a competition: Who could pay it forward the best?

Is there a problem in making a contest of something that ideally has no strings attached? Is it the same when there's a winner and a reward? Is it just human nature to seek to outdo others in anything and everything, including this? How does one measure altruism anyway?

Egolessness

There's a lot said nowadays about the ego, and we've spent some time looking at it already. The idea of late is to make ourselves somehow "egoless." As I described earlier, however, this part of our psyche serves a function, which is to mitigate the base urges of the id (including libidinal drives) by finding some socially acceptable way they can be acted out. The ego also mitigates the demands of the superego, which seeks perfection and usually finds the urges of the id reprehensible. The superego is the source for all moral restrictions. So do away with the ego, and we must do away with the id and superego—or must we?

What exactly is meant by an egoless state? Is that a state of denial? The principal human drives exist in deep ascetics, even if they believe they've been overcome. Let the ascetic suffer a blow to the head that renders a state of amnesia, and the aches from the belly for food will set him to eating just as much and as regularly as anyone else. In other words, training is a mental state that doesn't erase the basic inherited evolutionary drives. Rather, the discipline appears to deny those drives. Is ego therefore deniable in the same way? If so, is this what's meant by an egoless state?

A Healthy Ego

There are special people in history who have seemed to find an ego that was healthy rather than denied. Take Mother Teresa, for example—winner of the Nobel Peace Prize, but more important, the winner of nearly everyone's admiration. Tirelessly, she worked to ennoble the human race. In 1948, she observed the poor and starving beyond the walls of her community in Calcutta. She therefore sought and gained permission to leave the convent where she had been a teacher in order to work among the poorest of the poor. Her life was spent doing just that. In 1950, she obtained permission to establish the Missionaries of Charity. The society that grew from that group today performs charity work all over the globe. Mother Teresa knew who she was, and she possessed the ability to be herself and care for the poor and needy. Is she the icon for an egoless state?

I believe that the meaning intended by the word *egoless* is the suspension of the urges of the id in favor of the needs of others. It's actually a transcendence of the ego state. We might think of it as a rectified ego, meaning that this part of us is in perfect balance. The ego no longer seeks anything for its own purposes; it doesn't feel the need to win or to prove anything. From this perspective, it serves others not as an ego per se, but rather as one who shares with empathy the plight of all.

Perhaps this is a more natural state than we might think, for it's something most of us have experienced from time to time. This rectified ego recognizes the pain and suffering of others with great compassion and is compelled to go to the aid of those in need. It's the charity of the heart that demonstrates this possibility, even if only for a moment. The rectified ego can also be seen in the heart of one who simply chooses to do his best, to make the world a brighter place for others. Perhaps it is manifest in the artist who does his best to bring beauty into this world, or the cashier at the grocery store who always tries to bring a smile to everyone she meets. Maybe it's simply an altruistic ego?

A Rectified Ego

Was the boy in *Pay It Forward* correct in assuming that there's goodness in human nature? If charity and helping are goodness, then the answer is yes. Not only does this faculty exist, but it's hardwired in the human brain. Indeed, modern technology has demonstrated that there are areas in the brain dedicated to acting as "reward centers." Further, when human beings give to a charity or do good deeds for others, these centers are activated and good-feeling chemicals are released. Helping and being inwardly rewarded for it is built into the system, that's all there is to it. The more time we spend eliciting responses from these reward centers, the more egoless we become—or is that true?

Mystics have taught throughout recorded history that it's impossible to do a truly altruistic deed. Why? They inform us that the more good we do for the world, the more good comes to us. It's like the statement in the Bible: "What you sow is what you reap." Of course, some of the rewards are stored up in heaven in order to address the earthly inequities of those who have dedicated their lives to helping others, only to suffer and die themselves,. Thus we have the biblical admonishment against taking credit for our good deeds here because then our reward is here and not in heaven.

If we're all going to die anyway, it seems to me that the only thing that matters for now is how we live. Since there are no guarantees as to how many tomorrows we might have, it follows that each day should be spent wisely. For me this means have a little fun, enjoy life, do no harm, love, and help others. In aiding others, we'll get our inner rewards from the brain, and if those atheists are all wrong, then we'll have stored up some treasure for the other side. As I said in *Choices and Illusions,* go for that warm-fuzzy feeling that helping others provides.

Getting More—at Any Cost

Alternatively, some might argue that going for the gusto is warranted. Selfishly, this means more fun, more sex—more and more and more. Think of this: Christmas is the time of year for celebrating the glory and joy that arises from the promise of eternal life. The world observes this holiday in honor of the birth of Jesus Christ, who died on the cross and was resurrected to free humankind of its sins, promising everyone life beyond mortal death. As such, it's the time for "peace on Earth and goodwill to men."

The season is full of merriment and sales. In 2008, a crowd assembled outside a Wal-Mart store in Valley Stream, New York. The excitement grew as the 5 A.M. opening neared. Someone at the front of the line, who'd been waiting for hours, taped up a sign: "Blitz Line Starts Here." The crowd became impatient and began pounding on the glass door. The glass shattered, and the crowd rushed through it in search of their bargains, knocking to the ground and then trampling to death Jdimytai Damour, aged 34.

What goes through a person's head at such times? If you weren't part of the mob, it's difficult to understand how that could possibly happen. If you were, the hysteria of the moment no doubt dulled your senses. Witnesses reported that the crowd acted like savages. Is this a new breed—Christmas savages? Peace on earth and goodwill to the barbarians?

Meaning can be difficult to come by in almost any area of life if we stop long enough to really look. What does it say about the human race when a bargain incites a mob like a person arousing the living dead in some horror film? It's an unmitigated feeding frenzy—but why?

The Four F's

Psychologists speak of the four drives, the four F's, that all animals respond to: fight, flight, feeding, and fornicating. I have long argued for a fifth drive in our modern world: "more." But I say, why not more helpful instead of more selfish? Look at the world around us, and try to tell me that more selfishness holds the answers to a better world for our children and ourselves. When I was younger, I tried to live by Tom T. Hall's country song "Faster Horses (The Cowboy and the Poet)." In the song, an old man at the bar is asked the secret of life, and he answers, "It's faster horses, younger women, older whiskey, and more money." I know this might sound good, but it doesn't make for a happy person.

Faster horses (or cars) and the rest don't make for a good life for the simple reason they're all about selfishness. This self-centered way of living has no inner reward center, and eventually it leads to loneliness. Who wants to be around a selfish human being?

Love and Acceptance

Again we find that our biology, the world around us, and science actually reveal a message to and for all of us. This time it's about the need we all have to be loved and accepted. Being alone is unnatural for the human condition. When we're isolated, our systems shrivel and die early, and that's a fact. Indeed, research shows that friends and family both lengthen life and increase its quality.

Our thinking process is a product of our organ brains building a slate upon which something can be written, like language, before thought can proceed. Because of this, our world and the way we're wired should get some attention in our attempts to understand ourselves and thereby glimpse some aspect of humanity.

Religious centers in the brain,[1] reward centers for good deeds wired into it,[2] Bell's theorem,[3] and so much more suggest that to be true to myself, I must know first the difference between who I really am and who I think I am. To do that, I must evaluate how I think and where my thoughts come from. In so doing, it becomes incumbent on me to separate the content foisted upon me by others from what's original to me. No easy task—but then, I have a lifetime to do this. What does that mean?

170

chapter 24

SYNTHESIS

"The world is not dialectical—it is sworn to extremes,
not to equilibrium; sworn to radical antagonism, not to
reconciliation or synthesis. This is also the principle of evil."
— Jean Baudrillard

There's a statement in science based on mathematical proofs that simply declares: "All first principles are inherently unprovable." I'll take this up a bit later in more detail, but for our purposes here, I've found that not only are first principles unprovable but synthesis is ineffable—incapable of being expressed in words.

What do I mean by that? When we find that special state of inner peace, that sense of internal balance that so much of this book has been about, it's an experience. Sometimes it lasts for only a moment and other times for days, but when it comes to explaining or describing the event, that special synthesis of inner wisdom and knowing, of just being who we are, the words aren't there. The experience simply doesn't lend itself to linguistic convention.

Thesis, Antithesis, Synthesis

Mystical experiences—those said to be "one with the One"—are ineffable. Perhaps this is the case for the One within one—the divine within the individual—as well. For in this state of special inner balance, the true synthesis of thesis and antithesis, this place where opposites converge and blend just as two colors form a third, there's only the ineffable whole.

The practice known as *jnâna yoga* is a discipline of the intellect. Using the mind, we can evaluate so-called opposing perspectives, arguments of extreme opposites. One is thesis and the other antithesis, and where they converge, they may be depicted as an isosceles triangle (one with two equal sides). The point of convergence, or synthesis, sometimes exposes the opposites as being inherently flawed in such a way as to discharge the argument altogether. Many of the differences people struggle with then become totally irrelevant!

In *The God Theory* (which I quoted earlier), Bernard Haisch, Ph.D., a respected scientist, the author of more than 130 scientific publications, the former editor of the *Journal of Scientific Exploration,* and more, says something truly meaningful about knowing:

> We only understand what we are prepared to understand and, in today's world, public emphasis is on scientific, technological, and business knowledge, not esoteric truth. For those who have an active religious life—those who attend churches, pray in synagogues, or worship in temples—the emphasis is primarily on cultivating a personal relationship with the divine, not inquiring systematically into the nature of the spiritual world. The detailed investigation of reality has been turned over to science. Unfortunately the current paradigms of science exclude consideration of anything spiritual. In a vicious cycle of exclusion, modern science, the champion of objective inquiry, excludes the esoteric as an object susceptible of investigation. In doing so, science has abrogated its responsibility to uncover objective truth and succumbed to a dogmatism of its own.[1]

It's obvious that our world invalidates the subjective, because a subjective experience can't be independently verified and therefore lacks scientific credibility. Not only is that an example of a vicious cycle of exclusion, as Haisch terms it, but it's also a circular argument for "dumbness." It is indeed a dumbing down of everything that originally gave rise to our Greco-Western scientific culture. Whether we look to Socrates or Aristotle, Pythagoras or Ptolemy, science wasn't designed to obscure the big questions, let alone ignore or deny them altogether. Indeed, most of the great scientists have used their work to better understand their role in the universe and, in particular, their role with the divine.

chapter 25

MAGIC BULLET

"The magic bullet for everything is spelled <u>intentional effort.</u>"
— **Eldon Taylor**

In my experience, many people today seek instant gratification—not just in the classical sense of economics, but also in the realm of spiritual insight or enlightenment. They want "it" right now!

I'm often bemused by some who seem to be junkies of every spiritual or self-improvement guide out there but complain vociferously about the same old, same old. One case where I've seen this has to do with a response to one of my publishers, Hay House. I've seen repeated reviews by readers, some about my own work, who assert something like this: "Same old Hay House stuff—more forgiveness and the like."

Cognitive Dissonance

"Same old, same old" is usually something people think of in the context of day-to-day life, not their spiritual paths. If boredom and dissatisfaction are what they truly feel, then why do they keep buying the "same old, same old"? I think the issue is one of dissonance—that is, at some level the complaining readers are aware that the material, if followed, offers at least some clue to a beneficial spiritual direction, but they refuse to accept the essential tenet.

Cognitive dissonance isn't unusual in our society. Many individuals hold two mutually exclusive points of view, and they often fail to recognize this. I've had conversations in which these people have challenged the power of forgiveness, even calling the notion "grace." I've then asked them if they believe in grace, and they've affirmed that they do—all the while clinging tightly to the belief that they were victims in some way and forgiveness isn't always appropriate. But the very principle of grace is forgiveness. We see this in the biblical story of the prodigal son. When the young man finally recognized his error and returned, contrite, to his father's house, he was immediately welcomed as though he'd never left—forgiven as though forgiveness had never been necessary.

A Quick Fix

How is it that so many people today want a quick fix, an instant solution, the immediate answer, or the "magic bullet"? The most enjoyable aspects of life are those that are a journey, even with the trials they bring. A reward that comes too easily is hardly a prize. Enlightenment, although trite in today's usage, is still all about transcending the mundane, the physical boundaries that bind our bodies, the intellectually programmed notions of limitation. It means the spiritual nobility of the truth in "knowing." But what is there to know?

We with a Western mind-set expect an answer to every question. Although we're aware of questions for which there really are no answers—such as "Which came first, the chicken or the egg?"—most of us persist in our expectations that a question deserves an answer. And just as persistently, we often ask questions that distract from or fail the test of a genuine inquiry because they're circular, such as the egg question or my favorite: "How high is up?"

Implicit Assumptions

We all have many implicit assumptions about life, our perceptions, our beliefs, and everything else that's perceived as knowable. We rely on these assumptions, as we must for many aspects of life, such as recognizing appropriate behavior. When we see inappropriate actions, we tend to think of them as being inherently wrong, rather than acknowledging that we're making a judgment—or more specifically, that that judgment was programmed into us by our societal beliefs. Most of us also fail to recognize the implicit nature of language. A common example of this is the notion of everyday descriptions. To say that a table is square assumes that it isn't rectangular or round. Still, many don't notice descriptions of this nature, and therefore follow-up questions that ask for both the length and the width of the table are regarded as curious to say the least. (A square presupposes that the length and the width are the same.)

How is it that thinking people can ignore the critical nature of inquiry and so easily cop to a simple—even oversimplified—answer? It may make them feel enlightened, but it's quite the opposite. Perhaps that's a partial explanation for why so many people today are addicted to a special form of perennial self-help. Not that that's all bad, it's just that at some point they must stop simply taking in information and begin acting on it, or it isn't helping them.

Ask the Questions

The Herbert Hesse novel *Siddhartha* tells the story of enlightenment. It isn't something a person can give to anyone else. As close as the greatest guru can come is to ask the questions that will lead us inward to search for meaning. This quest is the journey. The answer isn't out there—trite but true. Instead, it's within each of us. We don't get there by meditation alone, though, and that's why there are so many different yogas. In our modern world, one full of continual informational stimulation, the yoga of the intellect begins by questioning assumptions—all of them. One-liners, quips, sound bites, and the like typically fall very short of truth.

The Price of Unconditional Love

A friend of mine has a son who's totally spoiled. He attends a private school and has every big-boy toy a young teenager can legally possess. He's never held a job or had to work for anything and expects to be doted upon by both his mother and his father. His personal habits aren't so different from those of many teenagers, so we can add to the mix a messy room and a certain amount of defiance. In this case, however, there's also an apparent lack of appreciation for everything he has. Therefore, it's treated accordingly—tossed here and there in a helter-skelter fashion.

The other day, my friend told me how hurt he was when his son called him a bastard. I learned that the boy used that name when his dad asked why he needed more money for one lunch than the $33 he was already carrying.

I know this man and his son, and the boy has never received corporal punishment or, in fact, serious discipline of any kind. The father, on the other hand, came from an abusive family and knew very well the pains of both emotional and physical punishment from his own parents. Additionally, my friend grew up in a low-income family that accepted church welfare when things got really tough. In his attempt to give his son everything he'd wanted as a child—the objects, the love, the affection, the attention, and the support—has he done the boy irreparable harm? That was his question to me.

Loving unconditionally is something most parents tend to do naturally with their children. So is the father wrong to try to give everything to his son?

We're all children in the sense that Jesus taught, sons and daughters of the Grand Organizing Designer (GOD). Do we expect that everything will just be given to us irrespective of our actions, our gratitude, our respect, and so forth? Is there a difference between what we expect from our parents and our children versus what we expect from God? Should there be?

Is there a quick fix for my friend's spoiled father-and-son relationship? Probably not—in fact it would be head-in-the-sand thinking to think there is. Is it now normal and acceptable for a son to call his father a bastard?

When I grew up, there was no such thing as children suing their parents, nor were there social workers yanking children from homes because some third party asserted the children were being mistreated. Has our society advanced when we give many parenting controls to teachers, schools, government, and so on? Should parents use corporal punishment more?

Peeling Back the Layers

In case you haven't gathered, I love Hesse's *Siddhartha* story. The title character has a son who disrespects him and eventually runs away. Siddhartha has learned peace, for he's gained that special solace recognized by others and labeled enlightenment. Still, his son wants no part of this, and the father finds once again that the peace he thought he'd gained was subject to another level of insight or enlightenment.

Our experience tempers our learnings. It defines the questions we ask—or should ask. And then the answers come through our further experiences. I once asked: "Is there really a God?" Events in my life, many of which I've shared in these pages, say to me in an irrefutable voice: "Absolutely!"

I'm convinced that every one of us, if we stop long enough to ask, to look, to search within—and if we pay attention to our lives—is given both the questions and the answers. The fact that you're reading this book suggests that you're inquiring as well. What are you asking? What are you being told? What does that mean?

chapter 26

TIMELINES AND MEMORY

"After all, a man's real possession is his memory.
In nothing else is he rich, in nothing else is he poor."
— **Alexander Smith**

When asked, most people describe their real selves as existing either in the mind or as consciousness in and out of the mind. It sounds complicated at first, but if we think about it for a minute, we realize that all of us think of our *selves,* our identities, if you will, as somewhere in our heads. Our consciousness is who we are, at least for most of us. As such, our personality, our memories, and everything else that makes up who we are is a heady matter (pun intended). So what happens if we lose our ability to think or much of our memories? Who are we then to ourselves?

These questions were relevant when I was asked to review *A Matter of Panache,* by Debra Sanders. Her memoir tells the story of how she lost much of her memory and ability to think as a result of head injuries suffered in an automobile accident.[1] It's a great read, and it set me thinking. In one part of the book, Debra informs the readers that she had to ask people she once had relationships with what had happened between them.

Who Are You Without Your Memory?

Imagine that you remember some significant other, but your recollection cuts off before the relationship ended—years before. In fact, your last memory is of a wonderful and loving exchange between the two of you. Imagine having to ask what happened to end the bond and somehow getting your feelings to square with your head and your current memories, as in today or yesterday. Who are you if you wake up one morning and know little of yourself?

Our memory, our timeline, is who we are—or is it? I know who I am in part because I know what I did to get to today. I know where I went to school, who my friends were, where I work, who my wife is, and so forth. I know my dog's name and his peculiar cries when I leave him unattended. I can name my favorite music, movies, television shows, and so on, so I think that I know something about myself.

Since this book is about *truly* knowing the self, I could add that I also have experiences that attest to a life after death, divine intervention, and more. I understand the dark side and have had at least one dark night of the soul. Based on this, I think I know a little more about myself, including the vast amount that I simply don't have a clue about—can't even take an educated guess at. So what if suddenly I have no memory, no yesterday or last night, such as the knowledge that I went to bed around 10 P.M., and here I am?

Imagine waking up in a strange place to a stranger—yourself. You don't even know until you try whether you're right- or left-handed. In fact, it takes little more effort to imagine not even knowing what handedness is. Just a bit more imagination, and you could wake up without a memory of everything you've learned, including your language. Now what do you have?

I'm sure you've realized that what we've ended up with is essentially a newborn, only perhaps one who's six feet tall and more than a few minutes old. That in and of itself is worthy of some thought, for it's an intriguing idea to think of memory as our identification. What if there is some mechanism that starts memory all over when we're born? We'll look at this more later on.

Just Being

Back to the original point: Who am I if I have no memory of who I am? Is memory critical to our being? The answer is obviously no, for many people throughout history have experienced amnesia, partial and otherwise, and they were all beings. Is memory more like an anchor that keeps us from moving into new ways of existing? I remember, for example, that public speaking can make me very nervous, so I avoid much of it. What if I didn't recall such self-imposed limitations?

What if in losing my memory, I gained the ability to experience and learn all over again, and in doing so I never experienced the same failures or fears? Would I still be the same person? The answer, again, is probably not. Would my personality be different if this were so? At the very least, the compensation mechanisms would be different and, I tend to believe, so would the personality.

Who am I then, if I'm not my memories? And if I *am* my memories, can I change the ones I choose? If so, I want only positive, reinforcing messages that encourage me to succeed at everything I enjoy or love. Isn't this the exact thing we want for our children?

Somehow I sense, even know in a certain way, that the aspect that *is* me is still there, even if I don't remember who that is. What I also somehow know is that within each of us is the ability to rewrite memory in favorable ways that empower us to improve and to reach new vistas in our search for meaning and exploration of life. Indeed, I'm convinced that if we forget about ourselves, our past, and restrictions or limitations that are often self-imposed, and instead turn our thoughts to other people, real insight into who we are and what we're made to do becomes obvious.

In helping others, we experience a neurochemical reward (apparently we were wired this way) and that quintessential sense I just call "the warm-fuzzy feeling." Additionally, we know that individuals in constant pain feel no discomfort when they go to the aid of another in need. It's almost as if we're factory built for service to our fellow human beings, and that in freely providing that service, we find we're actually rewarded with all of those good neurochemicals that make us feel happy.

Built to Experience Happiness

Without our memories, we're still wired to experience happiness. We don't need to want anything per se, such as the objects many people think will give them happiness. No, all we need to experience true joy is another human being, because we all have the opportunity to do something that helps that person, and our nature is this: with every piece of assistance we give, a reward is returned.

Memory—timelines—you're much more than just that. What do you think? What does that say to you? What does that mean?

chapter 27

THE SUBJECTIVE

"We can escape the commonplace only by manipulating it, controlling it, thrusting it into our dreams or surrendering it to the free play of our subjectivity."
— **Raoul Vaneigem,** philosopher

This book has been all about the stuff that's most dear to our hearts. Who are we? What is life, and what does it mean? Is there a purpose? Is there a God? Are we the product of some cosmic joke or accident? How do we answer these questions and the host of others that arise when we seriously look at the meaning of life?

In my opinion, there are no quick and easy answers that will satisfy everyone. Obviously, I'm convinced that life is meaningful, purposeful, and the result of a creative act by a Grand Organizing Designer (GOD). My personal experience has repeatedly made clear to me that such explanations as coincidence and the like are flatly inadequate. At the same time, I've found some of the so-called truisms of religious and spiritual systems—including the New Age movement—to be shallow, false, and otherwise disappointing. What then?

What anything means with regard to the value of life, its purpose, and so forth, is ultimately a subjective question. Experience is also intrinsically unquantifiable.

Ineffable experiences are clearly specific to each individual, and even if they could be articulated, for some the words would just be so much spiritual hyperbole. Closed minds don't open easily. It occurs to me that my life is as inherently subjective for me as yours is for you. How on earth can I know myself in some objective manner? I can know my behavior, but then I must ask: Why? This leads back into my head, my mind or consciousness, my understanding of me. My pain is mine—my hurts, angers, and loves are mine, and on and on. They can't truly be shared, because they're inside me. It isn't possible for me to open myself totally to another, even when I try. And if I really attempted to get everything out in the open, my defense mechanisms and the sum total of a lifetime of programming by media, culture, parents, and so forth, would still prevent me from fully sharing myself.

My Inner Self

Irish poet Thomas Moore said, "I think we would be able to live in this world more peaceably if our spirituality were to come from looking not just into infinity but very closely at the world around us— and appreciating its depth and divinity."

If I can share a glass of milk or a bowl of cereal, an apple or a pear, and laughter, then why can't I share my inner self? The answer for most people is simple—they don't know themselves. I've tried to illuminate some of the confusions, the theses and antitheses that have disturbed me. Much nonsense is spread around these days, like a label that looks attractive but says something quite different from what the onlooker expects. Still, I know that I've been unable to convey my innermost self, not only for the reasons I've already set out, but also because the entire process is merely the tip of the proverbial iceberg. I've therefore chosen to just continue asking the question: What does that mean?

chapter 28

THE CROWD WITHIN

"Reality leaves a lot to the imagination."
— **John Lennon**

It's easy to think of the world as being describable in more or less exact terms. Indeed, in a way, that is exactly what our sciences try to do. For example, we learn that the sun is a luminous celestial body composed mainly of hydrogen and helium and that hydrogen is a nonmetallic element, the lightest of all elements, and a highly flammable diatomic gas. Further, we learn that helium is an inert gas often used to blow up balloons that float into the air. With those definitions in place, we have a static view of things, and we also have the notion that we now know what they are.

We do not really know what something is just because we can name and describe it; and even if we did, it wouldn't remain the same simply because the world isn't a static place. As Heraclitus said, the world is in motion—constant flux. Everything is changing. The universe is dynamic, and so are you.

I once heard psychologist Robert Ornstein suggest that the steady, stable nature of personality so many cling to is probably false. I agree. The fact is, we're all many personalities rolled into one. We don't have multiple personality disorder, just different traits for different situations, social gatherings, environments and so forth. Therefore we can't accurately think of ourselves in a way that yields a steady state.

Changing Identity

When I put on my cowboy boots, Levi's, and Stetson, something more than just my clothes changes. I become a horseman in my mind, and my body adopts that posture. Sometimes when I dismount a horse, I notice that I walk with my toes turned in, like someone who has spent a lifetime on horseback, but when I'm wearing my Florsheim wing tips, that's never the case. Something else shifts, too: my vocabulary.

The first time I heard my father use "the F word" was in a garage where he was speaking to an auto mechanic friend of his. He'd forgotten I was there, and his language changed. My word choices are different, too, when I have a wrench in my hand and grease under my fingernails.

Wearing a three-piece suit or even a shirt and tie, I find that my behavior is different from when I'm around horses or in the garage. Put on athletic shoes and jeans and it changes some again. Why? The fact is that we all have many personalities, and each has its own body language and even sometimes clothing. Think about your posture. When you stick out your jaw, what goes on in your mind? When you puff up your chest or push it out and suck in your waist, what are you thinking? When you slouch, why do you do so, and what are your thoughts?

The psychology of the body is reflected in the mind, and there's mind-to-body reciprocation. Some people think of themselves as static. They believe that they know themselves well, but how many are honest about everything? Oh, perhaps they're up front with respect to the legal system, but do they ever lie? Would it be a falsehood to tell your badly injured mother that your father was still alive when you knew he'd died in the automobile accident that had put her in the hospital? Is it a lie to tell your children there is a Santa Claus? You see, we all lie about something.

Reconciling Ourselves

Give this some thought: Is there any human being who's truly nonviolent through and through? Is this person a pacifist to the degree that he'd stand aside while his child was slowly and deliberately tortured to death? Just as with our personalities, no attribute is static either. We may think of ourselves as peaceful, loving people, but there are limits to those characteristics as well. There is within all of us, I suspect, some evil as well as some good. Perhaps it's the reconciliation of the two that leads us to synthesis.

Your journey through this book has meant that you asked many questions and raised even more. Perhaps, like Siddhartha in Herman Hesse's novel, the answer isn't in a teaching, word, or description. In fact, the answer cannot be expressed. It isn't in one thing or anything, but rather in *everything* that we know "what is." That which we seek is defined by what it isn't, for it isn't ordinary and doesn't always fit conveniently into scientific or other belief paradigms. It just is.

It's in our experience, and we all know it in some way. Like consciousness itself, it just exists. No elucidation of detail can do justice to what is, for in the very act of describing the process we lose the real meaning. We must experience and then remember to know what is. And this is the path to the beginning of enlightenment: recognizing and remembering the what is. That's what it's all about.

❖❖❖ ❖❖❖

chapter 29

CONCLUSION OR NEW BEGINNING?

"There are two mistakes one can make along the road to truth . . .
not going all the way, and not starting."
— **Siddhartha Gautama,** founder of Buddhism

There's a Sufi story about the book of the book. Indeed, there's a volume by Idris Shah called *The Book of the Book,* and it appears to be about 300 pages. I bought it via mail order and discovered that 99 percent of it was blank. I did not return it, for it was well worth every penny I paid. Let me tell you why.

There's a saying about books that's also attributed to the Sufi. Paraphrased, it simply states: "It's not what the book says, but what the book does that matters." These are quite different things, when you think about it.

Shah's book tells the story of a sacred text that only the ruler can see.[1] The bottom line of the story comes down to the secret writings in this large, important-looking, leather-bound ancient text, held only for the ruler's eyes. And what did the entire book say? "When you know the difference between the container and the contents, you know all."

White Crows

To know the difference between the container and the contents, we must truly learn about both. I'm certain that you've remembered things in your life while reading this book that demonstrate what psychologist William James dubbed the "white crow." What James meant is that if an axiom states that all crows are black, all you need do is find one white crow to invalidate it. My life has had many white crows. Many of my experiences aren't easily dismissed, nor do they fit within the rules or axioms we know as science.

Some people teach that when we come into this life, a veil is drawn. Behind it is the information that could tell us why we're here, where we came from, how many times we might have made journeys of this type, and more. The veil protects us from this information so that we have the potential to develop in ways we might not otherwise. The barrier is said to serve many other functions, but for our purposes here, as a metaphor, it may be just what we continue to hide behind throughout our lives when we ignore events that speak to another reality, or at least another level of reality.

For me, asking the question "What if everything I believed was fake?" has merit. What about you? What would it mean to you if you discovered some or all of what you held true was indeed false?

Share the Journey

I'm not special by any means. Early in this book I shared a letter from a reader about her experience in heavy traffic, where she should have been hit by a truck coming down the freeway on-ramp, but instead found herself simply driving down the road. I've spoken to people around the world who've had experiences that quite simply insist on reminding us that here-and-now is not all there is.

I hope this book provokes something inside you that gives rise to a fundamental shift, "doing something" in the sense of the Sufi belief that "it is what a book does and not what it says that matters." I'd love to hear your experiences. Please leave them for me as comments on my Website: **http://www.eldontaylor.com.**

This should be just a beginning. As you've read, I was often just too busy with life to follow through with many of my experiences. Perhaps I could have had an Indiana Jones–type of adventure if I'd been paying attention. I don't let things pass me by anymore; now I make sure I pay attention.

I don't want you to be so busy that you, too, ignore or pass by opportunities or new awareness, for these insights are really the small but sure access points we have to "knowing" ourselves and the meaning of life. I trust that the trite "same old, same old" saying is no longer a part of your expectation or thought pattern. To that end, take a moment and look again at what you've questioned.

This is the beginning, and that's all it can be. If you'd like to continue on this journey with me, please go to **www.eldontaylor .com** and subscribe to my free newsletter. I look forward to hearing from you.

❖❖❖ ❖❖❖

Epilogue

There's a cute television show called *Are You Smarter than a Fifth Grader?* The producers actually give a couple of mental-fitness examinations to potential participants, one of which is a basic intelligence (IQ) test. Some participants have tested in the very gifted area, yet they've had to admit they weren't smarter than a fifth grader.

Life is full of questions: What does this mean? What does that mean? Why am I here? What's the meaning of life? Who am I?

On and on they go, and the wonderful thing is that as long as there are questions, there's a game. Think of it this way: What happens when the inquiries cease? In all question-based games, when the asking ends, the game is over.

Life is about wonder, and the meaning is often in the question, not the answer! When we have all the solutions, there's no reason for the game to continue. It's really that simple.

That's not to suggest that we don't have some answers, some partial meaning. Obviously, we know many things. Still, what I mean to suggest is that only by noticing and then asking do we really discover anything about ourselves as individuals.

Great questions are just that. Although some may have been around so long that they provoke—as my favorite English teacher once suggested—such a trite response as to have Adam kick the slats out of his cradle, they nevertheless remain great questions simply because they haven't been fully resolved. So the question "Who am I?" is as valid today as it has ever been. What's more, pat answers to the mysteries of life are typically blatantly oversimplified fairy tales. As John Wisdom is said to have remarked, they may make you "feel good, as in having Daddy at the end of the hall when you have a bad dream," but this passes quickly under scrutiny in the light of day.

They say success is a journey, not a destination. *Life* is a journey, and the meaning to life is that path. The questions we ask along the way become the tools that assist us in navigating a course, as opposed to drifting asleep at the wheel. We live in a time when more and more people are awakening, and that isn't happening any too soon. It's my hope that in some way this book has contributed to the dialogue that's essential if the world is ever to become so fully awake that peace, balance, and harmony exist for all people as a normal way of life.

Thanks for reading and all the best,
Eldon

❖❖❖ ❖❖❖

Acknowledgments

First, I must acknowledge my son Preston Bryce Taylor, who has shown great interest in the matters contained in this work and with whom I've enjoyed many delightful discussions. I must also recognize my lovely wife, Ravinder, who works tirelessly, seeing to every minute detail in my manuscripts, especially that tedious task called a Bibliography. I also wish to recognize and express my appreciation for my longtime friend and editor Suzanne Brady. She brings much more than editing skills to the table, but if editing has an archetype, Suzanne is it.

Advancement comes only on the shoulders of many who have come before, marked out their specialty, delivered their epistles, spoken their soliloquies, written their classic works, debated their metaphysical foundations, philosophized about being and nothingness, sanitized their sciences, modeled their mathematics, and so much more. It goes without saying that to them—all of them—I owe a great debt.

It's with deep humility that I continue to enjoy the great works of so many others while I strive to develop my own small contribution. This result would be nothing at all without the minds that went before me, including the One Mind behind it all.

✧✧✧   ✧✧✧

Endnotes

Chapter 4

1. Krippner, S.; Wickramasekera, I.; Wickramasekera, J. & Winstead, C. W. III. 1998. "The Ramtha phenomenon: Psychological, phenomenological, and geomagnetic data." *Journal of the American Society for Psychical Research,* 92(1), pp. 1–24.

2. Guillory, W. 2001. *The Living Organization: Spirituality in the Workplace.* Salt Lake City, UT: Innovations International, Inc.

3. Guillory, W. 1996. *The Guides.* Medical Lake, WA: R. K. Books.

4. Jung, C. J. 2005. *Four Archetypes: Mother, Rebirth, Spirit, Trickster.* 3rd edition. New York: Routledge Classics.

5. Hyde, J. 2004. "1984 Lafferty Case Still Haunts." *Deseret News.* Salt Lake City, UT. June 24, 2004.

6. Ibid.

Chapter 5

1. Deal, D. C. & Cook, W. 2003. *Incidents Beyond Coincidence.* Hope, ID: WynLora Publishing.

2. Springer, S. P. and Deutsch, G. 1981. *Left Brain Right Brain.* New York: Freeman and Co.

3. Swann, I. 1993. *Your Nostradamus Factor.* New York: Fireside.

4. Jaynes, J. 2000. *The Origin of Consciousness and the Breakdown of the Bicameral Mind.* New York: Mariner Books.

5. Baird, F. E. and Kaufmann, W. 2008. *From Plato to Derrida.* Upper Saddle River, NJ: Pearson Prentice Hall.

6. Descartes, R. 2007. *Cogito, Ergo Sum: The Life of Rene Descartes.* Edited by Richard Watson. Boston, MA: David R. Godine.

7. Kant, I. 1965. *Immanuel Kant's Critique of Pure Reason.* New York: St. Martin's Press.

Chapter 6

1. Tolle, E. 2008. *A New Earth: Awakening to Your Life's Purpose.* New York: Penguin.

2. Schopenhauer, A. 2006. *The Essays of Arthur Schopenhauer: the Wisdom of Life.* Lenox, MA: Hard Press.

3. Emerson, R. W. 1908. *The Essay On Self-Reliance.* Whitefish, MT: Kessinger Publishing.

4. Tolle, E. 2008. *A New Earth: Awakening to Your Life's Purpose.* New York: Penguin.

5. Penfield W. 1955. "The Role of the Temporal Cortex in Certain Psychical Phenomena." *Journal of Mental Science,* 1955. 101:451–65.

Chapter 7

1. Associated Press. 2008. *Conn. Police Release 911 Calls in Hit-And-Run.* http://www.msnbc.msn.com/id/25010977/.

2. Ibid.

3. Milgram, S. 1963. "Behavioral Study of Obedience." *Journal of Abnormal and Social Psychology, 67,* 371–378.

4. Associated Press. 2008. *Tape Shows Woman Dying on Waiting Room Floor.* http://www.cnn.com/2008/US/07/01/waiting.room.death/index .html.

Chapter 9

1. Libet, B., et al. 1967. "Unconscious Process and the Evoked Potential." *Science,* 158, p. 1597, and Soon, C. S.; Brass, M.; Heinze, H. & Haynes, J. 2008. "Unconscious Determinants of Free Decisions in the Human Brain." *Nature Neuroscience,* 11, 543–545. As cited by: Hotz, R. 2008. "Get Out of Your Own Way." *Wall Street Journal,* June 27, A9. **http://online.wsj. com/public/article_print/SB121450609076407973.html.**

2. Crabtree, V. 2006. "Split Brain Studies: One Mind per Hemisphere." **http://www.humantruth.info/split_brain.html.**

3. Shevrin, H. 1984–2006. *Subliminal Communication Technology Committee on Science and Technology U.S. House of Representatives.* Honolulu, HI: University Press of the Pacific.

4. Gazzaniga, M. S. 2008. "Spheres of Influence." *Scientific American Mind.* June/July, pp. 33–39.

5. Seligman, M. E. P. 1995. *What You Can Change and What You Can't.* New York: Fawcett Book.

6. Ibid.

Chapter 12

1. Haisch, B. 2006. *The God Theory.* San Francisco, CA: Weiser Books.

2. Jung, C. G. 1981. *The Archetypes and The Collective Unconscious (Collected Works of C.G. Jung Vol.9 Part 1).* Princeton, NJ: Princeton University Press.

3. Sheldrake, R. 1995. *The Presence of the Past: Morphic Resonance and the Habits of Nature.* Rochester, VT: Park Street Press.

Chapter 13

1. Marks, D. & Kammann, R. 1980. *The Psychology of the Psychic.* Amherst, NY: Prometheus Books.

2. Ibid.

Chapter 15

1 . Descartes, R. 2007. *Cogito, Ergo Sum: The Life of Rene Descartes.* Edited by Richard Watson. Boston, MA: David R. Godine.

Chapter 16

1. Taylor, E. 2007. *Choices and Illusions: How Did I Get Where I Am and How Do I Get Where I Want to Be?* Carlsbad, CA: Hay House.

2. Harrison, D. M. 1999. "Bell's Theorem." **http://www.upscale .utoronto.ca/PVB/Harrison/BellsTheorem/BellsTheorem.html** and Albert, D. Z. & Galchen, R. 2009. "Bell's Theorem and the Physical World." *Scientific American.* **http://www.sciam.com/article.cfm?id=bells-theorem.**

3. Jauregui, A. 2007. *Epiphanies.* New York: Beyond Words.

Chapter 17

1. Foundation for Inner Peace. 1996. *The Course in Miracles.* New York: Viking.

Chapter 20

1. Jaynes, J. 2000. *The Origin of Consciousness and the Breakdown of the Bicameral Mind.* New York: Mariner Books.

2. Libet, B., et al. 1967. "Unconscious Process and the Evoked Potential." *Science,* 158, p. 1597, and Soon, C. S.; Brass, M.; Heinze, H. & Haynes, J. 2008. "Unconscious Determinants of Free Decisions in the Human Brain." *Nature Neuroscience,* 11, 543–545. As cited by: Hotz, R. 2008. "Get Out of Your Own Way." *Wall Street Journal,* June 27, A9. **http://online.wsj. com/public/article_print/SB121450609076407973.html.**

3. Jung, C. J. 2005. *Four Archetypes: Mother, Rebirth, Spirit, Trickster.* 3rd edition. New York: Routledge Classics.

Chapter 22

1. Seligman, M. E. P. 2006. *Learned Optimism: How to Change Your Mind and Your Life.* New York: Vintage.
2. Harrison, D. M. 1999. "Bell's Theorem." http://www.upscale .utoronto.ca/PVB/Harrison/BellsTheorem/BellsTheorem.html and Albert, D. Z. & Galchen, R. 2009. "Bell's Theorem and the Physical World." *Scientific American.* http://www.sciam.com/article.cfm?id=bells-theorem.
3. Bower, B. 2008. "Body in Mind." *Science News.* October 25, 2008.
4. Libet, B., et al. 1967. "Unconscious Process and the Evoked Potential." *Science,* 158, p. 1597, and Soon, C. S.; Brass, M.; Heinze, H. & Haynes, J. 2008. "Unconscious Determinants of Free Decisions in the Human Brain." *Nature Neuroscience,* 11, 543–545. As cited by: Hotz, R. 2008. "Get Out of Your Own Way." *Wall Street Journal,* June 27, A9. http://online.wsj .com/public/article_print/SB121450609076407973.html.
5. Harrison, D. M. 1999. "Bell's Theorem." http://www.upscale .utoronto.ca/PVB/Harrison/BellsTheorem/BellsTheorem.html and Albert, D. Z. & Galchen, R. 2009. "Bell's Theorem and the Physical World." *Scientific American.* http://www.sciam.com/article.cfm?id=bells-theorem.

Chapter 23

1. Penfield W. 1955. "The Role of the Temporal Cortex in Certain Psychical Phenomena." *Journal of Mental Science,* 1955. 101:451-65.
2. Hinterthuer, A. 2007. "Can't Buy Me Altruism." *ScienceNOW Daily News,* June14, 2007. http://sciencenow.sciencemag.org/cgi/content/ full/2007/614/1.
3. Harrison, D. M. 1999. "Bell's Theorem." http://www.upscale .utoronto.ca/PVB/Harrison/BellsTheorem/BellsTheorem.html and Albert, D. Z. & Galchen, R. 2009. "Bell's Theorem and the Physical World." *Scientific American.* http://www.sciam.com/article.cfm?id=bells-theorem.

Chapter 24

1. Haisch, B. 2006. *The God Theory.* San Francisco, CA: Weiser Books.

Chapter 26

1. Sanders, D. 2008. *A Matter of Panache: A Career in Public Education. A Traumatic Brain Injury. A Memoir of Surviving Both.* Parker, CO: Outskirts Press.

Chapter 29

1. Shah, I. 1986. *The Book of the Book.* London, UK: Octagon Press.

InnerTalk Distribution

USA
Progressive Awareness Research, Inc.
PO Box 1139
Medical Lake, WA 99022
1-800-964-3551
1-509-244-6362
www.innertalk.com

UK
Vitalia Health
P. O. Box 2492
Marlow, Bucks SL7 2WW
UK
011 44 1628 898 366
www.innertalk.co.uk

Germany
Axent Verlag
Steinerne Furt 78
86167 Augsburg
Germany
011 49 821 70 5011
www.axent-verlag.de

Mexico
Dialogo Interno
Calle Retorno Cerro De Acazulco No. 6
Col. Oxtopulco Universidad Del. Coyoacan
Mexico D.F. C.P.04318
Mexico
011 52 555 339 5742
www.dialogointerno.com.mx

**Malaysia/Singapore/Brunei/Australia/
New Zealand/Papua New Guinea**
InnerTalk Sdn Bhd
2–2 Jalan Pju 8/5E, Perdana Bus. Cntr.
Bandar Damansara Perdana,
47820 Petaling Jaya
Selangor, Malaysia
011 60 37 729 4745
www.innertalk-au.com
www.innertalk.co.nz
www.innertalk.com.my

Taiwan and China
Easy MindOpen
3F, No. 257, Ho-Ping East Rd. Sec. 2
Taipei, Taiwan, R.O.C
011 886 (227) 010–468(1)
www.iamone.com.tw

Distribution Inquiries

For information about distributing InnerTalk programs, please contact

Progressive Awareness Research, Inc.
PO Box 1139
Medical Lake, WA 99022
1-800-964-3551
1-509-244-6362
www.innertalk.com

About the Author

Eldon Taylor has made a lifelong study of the human mind and has earned doctoral degrees in psychology and metaphysics. He's a fellow with the American Psychotherapy Association (APA) and a nondenominational minister.

A practicing criminalist for more than ten years while completing his education, Eldon supervised and conducted investigations and testing to detect deception. His earliest work with changing inner beliefs was conducted from this setting, including a double-blind study at the Utah State Prison from 1986 to 1987.

Eldon is president and director of Progressive Awareness Research, Inc. For more than 25 years, his books, audio programs, lectures, and radio and television appearances have approached personal empowerment from the cornerstone perspective of forgiveness, gratitude, self-responsibility, and respect for all life.

He lives in the countryside of Washington state with his wife and their two sons.

To Learn More about Eldon Taylor

If you've enjoyed this book and would like to learn more about tools to help you become the person you were meant to be, visit Eldon's Website: **http://www.eldontaylor.com.**

If you're interested in accessing more control over your self-talk and your own inner beliefs, you may wish to try Eldon's patented audio technology, known as InnerTalk. Independent researchers have repeatedly proved that InnerTalk is effective at changing thoughts and thereby influencing behavior in a variety of areas affecting our daily lives. You may download free samples of InnerTalk and find a large selection of self-improvement products by going to: **http://www .innertalk.com.**

To be informed about Eldon's latest research and work and to hear about special offers on Eldon's books and audio products, please subscribe to his free e-newsletter by going to: **http://www .eldontaylor.com.** You may also request a free catalog by calling 800-964-3551 or writing to Progressive Awareness Research, Inc., PO Box 1139, Medical Lake, WA 99022.

❖❖❖

Notes

Notes

Notes

Notes

Notes

Notes

Notes

Notes

Notes

✦✦✦ ✦✦✦

Hay House Titles of Related Interest

YOU CAN HEAL YOUR LIFE, the movie,
starring Louise L. Hay & Friends
(available as a 1-DVD program and an expanded 2-DVD set)
Watch the trailer at: **www.LouiseHayMovie.com**

THE SHIFT, the movie,
starring Dr. Wayne W. Dyer
(available as a 1-DVD program and an expanded 2-DVD set)
Watch the trailer at: **www.DyerMovie.com**

All You Ever Wanted to Know from His Holiness the Dalai Lama on Happiness, Life, Living, and Much More: Conversations with Rahjiv Mehrotra

The Biology of Belief: Unleashing the Power of Consciousness, Matter & Miracles, by Bruce H. Lipton, Ph.D.

Led by Faith: Rising from the Ashes of the Rwandan Genocide, by Immaculée Ilibagiza, with Steve Erwin

Personal Development for Smart People: The Conscious Pursuit of Personal Growth, by Steve Pavlina

Your Soul's Compass: What Is Spiritual Guidance, by Joan Borysenko, Ph.D., and Gordon Dveirin, Ed.D.

✦✦✦

All of the above are available at your local bookstore,
or may be ordered by contacting Hay House (see next page).

We hope you enjoyed this Hay House book.
If you'd like to receive our online catalog featuring additional
information on Hay House books and products, or if you'd like to find
out more about the Hay Foundation, please contact:

Hay House, Inc.
P.O. Box 5100
Carlsbad, CA 92018-5100

(760) 431-7695 or (800) 654-5126
(760) 431-6948 (fax) or (800) 650-5115 (fax)
www.hayhouse.com® • www.hayfoundation.org

Published and distributed in Australia by: Hay House Australia Pty. Ltd., 18/36 Ralph St., Alexandria NSW 2015 • *Phone:* 612-9669-4299 • *Fax:* 612-9669-4144 • www.hayhouse.com.au

Published and distributed in the United Kingdom by: Hay House UK, Ltd., 292B Kensal Rd., London W10 5BE • *Phone:* 44-20-8962-1230 • *Fax:* 44-20-8962-1239 • www.hayhouse.co.uk

Published and distributed in the Republic of South Africa by: Hay House SA (Pty), Ltd., P.O. Box 990, Witkoppen 2068 • *Phone/Fax:* 27-11-467-8904 • info@hayhouse.co.za • www.hayhouse.co.za

Published in India by: Hay House Publishers India, Muskaan Complex, Plot No. 3, B-2, Vasant Kunj, New Delhi 110 070 • *Phone:* 91-11-4176-1620 • *Fax:* 91-11-4176-1630 • www.hayhouse.co.in

Distributed in Canada by: Raincoast, 9050 Shaughnessy St., Vancouver, B.C. V6P 6E5 • *Phone:* (604) 323-7100 • *Fax:* (604) 323-2600 • www.raincoast.com

Take Your Soul on a Vacation

Visit **www.HealYourLife.com**® to regroup, recharge,
and reconnect with your own magnificence.
Featuring blogs, mind-body-spirit news, and life-changing
wisdom from Louise Hay and friends.

Visit **www.HealYourLife.com** today!

HEAL YOUR LIFE ♥

Take Your Soul on a Vacation

Get your daily dose of inspiration today at **www.HealYourLife.com®**. Brimming with all of the necessary elements to ease your mind and educate your soul, this Website will become the foundation from which you'll start each day. This essential site delivers the latest in mind, body, and spirit news and real-time content from your favorite Hay House authors.

Make It Your Home Page Today!

www.HealYourLife.com®

HAY HOUSE

www.hayhouse.com®